Sara Ratcliff has asserted her right und
and Patents act 1988 to be identified as the author of this work.

1ˢᵗ Edition 2020

This is a work of creative non fiction. The events are portrayed to the best of Sara Ratcliff's memory, While all the stories in this book are true, some names and identifying details have been changed to protect the privacy of the people involved.

ISBN: 978-1-5272-7650-5

Published by Marie Curtis Publications
email: mariecurtispublications@outlook.com

Cover photo courtesy of and gifted by Jason Kukalowicz

Edited by: Tony Ratcliff

Other books by this publisher you may be interested in:
Be Home Before it Gets Dark Son by Tony Ratcliff,
ISBN: 978 1 5272 3808 4

The Sky is my Witness, It Saw it All, by Tony Ratcliff and guest author Sara Ratcliff,
ISBN: 978 1 5272 3911 1

Manchester..More of my Life's Stories by Tony Ratcliff A Manc Lad Born and Bred
ISBN: 978 1 5272 7484 6

Thank you for obtaining our books. Hope you like them.

Page   Contents

Chapter One
My Beginning Years

One bright, sunny, spring morning back in the mid 1970's a little girl was born into a Northern England family called the Watsons. Who lived in Stockport not far from the infamous Quaffers nightclub.

Well this baby girl, ME, was born at home but it soon became apparent that there were some health problems with the new Mum, and with the baby. So they were both taken in to hospital. After treatment that lasted a few days we were both allowed home.

But my Dad, Alfred, was not too pleased at all as he wanted his wife Marie to have given birth to a little boy to carry on the family name. No gender reveal back then.

Dad had prepared a blue room expecting his new baby to be a son. "Arh well." He said to his brother Tommy, who was waiting there with him for us to arrive home in a taxi, "It'll do. I ain't re-painting that room again."

Then Mother and baby arrived home and all three settled down together in the living room. I was placed in a cot next to the kitchen door, not too far from the fire place. Now we lived on Hayfield Road in Bredbury, Stockport in a semi-detached ex-factory house that my Dad had not long since taken out a mortgage on.

Well Uncle Tommy kissed me on my head, and put a fifty pence piece in my hand. He said "Congrats!" to his brother Alfred and Marie, then went home to his house,

Alfred, my Dad and my Mum sat down to drink their cups of tea. When Dad sat down he lit his pipe as he usual did, and had done since the day they had moved in to this house. Then my Mum smacked her hand down hard on the arm of her chair saying loudly, "ALFRED! Not in front of the baby! No, there'll be no smoking in here now will there?"

"Whoops!" He said "No, Mar no." and promptly got up and emptied his pipe into the tin bin that was at the side of his chair. Then Dad went in to the kitchen and threw his pipe in to the kitchen drawer. He came back into the front room, saying,

"You settle down now Mar and have a rest. I'm off to the Con Club for a pint to celebrate with the lads, back soon Mar." Then off he went out the front door and off to his local Conservative Club, where he would play snooker and have a few goes on the one arm bandits in the club, till hunger would rumble in his belly then he would come home.

Now when he got home and they'd had something to eat, Dad and Mum had a chat about naming the baby. As the name Dad had picked for the baby, believing me to be a boy throughout the pregnancy, was Lee Alfred. This now had to be changed for when Dad would register the baby's birth and name at the local Registry office, as this new addition to the family was a baby girl.

It took both parents discussing and debating to finally come up with a name for me, the baby, that they were both happy with, which was Sarah Marie. Well as is tradition in the Watson family, the father would be the one to go and register the name and birth which Dad did. But as normal, Dad being Dad, decided to call me SARA not Sarah as agreed.

So when he returned home and showed the birth certificate to Mum, she was none too pleased with him. But Dad chirped up when Mum was complaining, "Well it'll be easier for her to spell when she gets older eh Mar?" He said chuckling to himself. "You're just a bugger!" Mar said, "I knew I married Mr. Right, but I didn't know his first name was Always!" Then she threw one of my rattles at him as he went into the kitchen to make a cup of tea and a sandwich.

Well the days rolled by into weeks and months and now I had started to crawl around the floor as babies do. Soon Dad, being Dad, started to complain. "Marie!" He'd shout, "Look! She's gone and done it again, she's knocked my cuppa over!"

Now Dad, not the baby, never learned and would always place his cup of tea, well pint pot of tea, on the floor at the side of his chair. And an ashtray on the arm of his chair for the ash out of his pipe. Yes you've got it, Alfred was now smoking his pipe in the living room again, as he always used to before I was born.

But he now had to contend with a high chair and a cot in the living room. As well as a pushchair folded up in the hallway for when Dad and Marie, my Mum, would take little, but growing fast, noisy and clumsy baby me out on visits to relatives and the shops. Also for when Dad sneakily took me out off into the games and arcade shops on Stockport precinct, while Mum would stay at home preparing meals and cleaning the house.

Now my Dad was a hard working man at the time and worked twelve hour shifts at Chadkirk Dye Works in Bredbury, Stockport. Therefore he only really spent his spare time at home of a weekend.

Though most Saturday evenings he would go down to Bredbury Conservative Club for a few pints of bitter with his pals and a couple of games of snooker. And he always had a dabble on the one arm bandit and the fruit machines while he was there. Over the years playing those fruit machines became a bad money losing habit for Dad.

So my earliest memories of time spent with my Dad are of him taking me to the arcades with him. As instead of taking me for a walk in the park as he told Mum, Dad now was using taking me out for a walk to hide the fact he was going in the arcades to play the fruit machines. This lasted a couple of years until one day I, now starting to string words together, told Mum of these flashing lights and ringing noises on the things Dad was playing with.

Well I won't repeat what happened but it wasn't pretty, nor were those words, so Dad taking me out soon stopped. Unfortunately Dad's habit of playing the fruit machines and losing money didn't.

Well my life rolled on as life does. Mum now started, when she could being a busy mother, taking me to the local parks herself. Whoopee! I loved my Mum pushing me on the swings and really enjoyed the rocking horses rides bobbing up and down.

And of course I loved having a go on the various roundabouts and playing in the sand pit with my little bucket and spade. But the one thing I hated and was petrified of was the slide. Even though Mum would just put me up at chest height at the bottom of the slide I would just screech out and cling to my Mum's neck, so the slides were a no no for me.

Then the big day came for me to start nursery. Well what can I say. Just like all other kids this was not the best of days, having to be separated from my loving Mum was a huge jolt and not a pleasant experience at all. It took a good few days and a lot of coaxing from the teacher and my Mum before finally I didn't scream the place down and settled in with the new friends I had now started to make and play with.

The first friend I made was a little girl named Helen Grundy. Soon after that, this once shy and only child made lots and lots of new friends.

My auburn hair now was getting really long and wavy for a girl my age, which now my Mum was plaiting for me each morning before school. And it wasn't just my hair that was growing, I soon became the tallest girl in the class. But something was sadly wrong as my writing, reading and spelling was not as good as the rest of the class.

Which made Dad angry and he started calling me a thick little ? . Well that goes without saying. Mum tried, along with my teacher, to take time out and try to help me with my school work. Also Mum tried to help me with reading books at home, like Janet and John, and The Adventure reading books. Which just annoyed Dad when he was at home as he was now working shift work hours in his new job at I.C.I. and was seldom at home when I was awake.

He also now started spending more and more time away from home on his days or nights off work. Dad seemed to be always down the Conservative Club, at the local arcades or out fishing the local canal and ponds. Sometimes Dad would also go to the club or pub with his other brother, my Uncle Ronald. He didn't seem to want to bond with little me at all, nor with Mum.

Now Mum had started to become poorly. So the park trips with her were now getting less and less as she became more and more poorly. Well I didn't realise just how poorly my Mum really was. And as children do I just played out in front of our house with some new found friends that lived locally.

Well Dad had a disused shed in the back garden of our house in Bredbury. I asked my Mum if me and my friends could play in this disused shed. Mum told me she would have a word with Dad next time she saw him. Which she did, but at first he said no. But my Mum kept on asking Dad and he finally gave in saying, "If they clean the thing out why not?"

Now this shed, though only small, was full of rubbish of every kind. Old pots and pans, old tools, bits of wood, old car parts from cars Dad repaired from time to time, old picture frames and so on.

Well now after me working, along with my friends, clearing the shed out bit by bit, disposing of all the rubbish in the bins over several weeks, finally the shed was cleared and now empty. Well me and my pals would soon have a place to play in the cold or wet weather.

My Mum got out of her now sick bed and gave the old shed a good hoovering out and cleaned the windows. Then Mum phoned and asked her cousin and good friend Reginald if he could paint the inside of the shed white and the outside brown, which he did over the next few days.

He wouldn't take any money for doing these jobs or for the paint. Reg told Mum, "That's what families are for." He also told Mum the door hinges were broken and the roof needed new roofing felt but he would come and sort them out in a few days as he had a job on decorating a house. As this is what Reginald did for a living, decorating and property repairs.

Then in the meantime I carried on playing on the front near our home with my pals, all of us talking as we played about the play shed we now called our home.

When Uncle Reg, as I called him, kept his word and called back about a week later and completed the jobs on the shed he asked Mum to come and inspect the shed and the work he had now completed. Mum was amazed how good the shed now looked.

Then Uncle Reg and Mum called me off the front and showed me the now new looking shed. Uncle Reg had even put a door number on the shed door. I took one look at the shed and the inside and asked, "Mum, Uncle Reg, is it really mine?" They answered, "Yes!" "Yippee!" I yelled, and ran onto the front and called my friends off the front saying, "Come and see! … Come and see! Please come and see, it's brilliant!" So four girls, Claire, Susan, Gillian and Katie, came round the back of our house to see the new shed and they too were amazed.

At this point Dad came home with a right mood on. Mum and I hadn't seen him for days now. He immediately saw the shed and said, "Hey Reg, it needs a lock putting on that thing." and just went in the house. Uncle Reg put a lock on the shed later that day and went to give Mum the keys. Dad yelled, "Give those keys to me Reg!" which Reg did and he said to Mum, "I'd best go." and he gave Mum a kiss on the cheek and left.

When Uncle Reg had gone Mum and Dad had a row about money and the shed. My Dad told Mum, "If that brat," meaning me, "wants to play in the shed and call it home she'll have to do what the rest of us do and pay rent. That'll come out of her spends. We all have to learn nowt's for nowt so I'll make her a rent book now. Those bloody kids she plays with are not allowed round the back, let alone in that shed! The noisy brats will just keep me awake." I was now about just eight years old.

My once vibrant, tough talking Mum had started

to become weaker, frail and pretty quiet, especially when Dad found the time to return home. I lost many of my friends that day as they had heard what my Dad had said about them not being allowed round our back garden, nor in the shed they had all worked so hard to clean out.

Though my Mum, still with a little fight left in her, when she knew my Dad was at work, would let the couple of friends I still had come round the back and play in the garden and the shed. But pretty soon after, the time flew by and the dark nights began to draw in and the cold weather and Jack Frost were knocking at the door. So not much playtime outside during these days.

Then Christmas arrived in what seemed a flash. Dad bought me a rag doll and Mum bought me a tea set to play in the shed with when the weather improved. I was so excited and played in the house in my bedroom with the tea set, pretending to be Mummy making imaginary dinners and cups of tea. I had no friends there to play with though, as Dad would never allow other children in the house at all. But I did make and have some friends at the junior school I was now attending, St. Mark's C. of E. so things weren't too bad for me during those days.

Chapter Two
The First Time I Saw the Sea

During the Easter break Dad's mother, my Grandma, and her sister Ada had gone on holiday to North Wales for a week in a caravan on Happy Days holiday camp.

During their holiday about mid week, they phoned Dad and asked him if he, my Mum and little me would like to come down and stay with them for a couple of days in the caravan they had rented, as it was an six berth caravan and was already paid for. So it wouldn't cost a penny, just food money and petrol money to get there was needed, and voila, a free holiday! Well surprisingly, Dad didn't say no. It was his Mother and Auntie though, and it could have caused trouble with them if he had said no. So after getting some things ready for the sea side our little family now popped off on our trip to sunny North Wales and Happy Days caravan park.

Now I had never ever been on a holiday. I must have driven Dad nuts on the trip there as I was so excited to go to the seaside. All my friends at school had been on holidays to the seaside and had told me all about their holidays.

So I asked Dad, "Will we see the sea?" "Will we see the beach?" "Will there be crabs?" "Will there be sea gulls?" "Can I make sand castles with a bucket and spade?" And so on ….. all the way there. All Dad could say was, "Shut that brat up will you Mar, I'm bloody driving and she's driving me nuts!" Mar just kept saying, "Shush you'll see when we get there." And to Dad she said, "Leave her alone, she's excited like any other child would be. Just leave her alone and stop calling her a brat." This all went on till we arrived at the caravan park.

Where I saw the sea for the first time as we drove into the camp to find Grandma's caravan. I said, "Whorrrr!" to Mum, "Isn't it big Mum, it goes all the way over there. And where does it end?" Dad said, "I wish you'd bloody end!" as we pulled up outside Grandma's caravan.

Dad turned the engine off and said, "You two wait here." He got out of the car and knocked on the caravan door. Then knocked again, harder this time, and said, "Bloody charmin' in it? All this way and they're not even in."

Well me and Mum were really hot and thirsty in the car and we guessed Dad was too. We all needed the loo, so off we popped to find the toilets and guess who we bumped into on our way to the toilets?

You got it, Grandma and her sister Ada who said, "Hello you lot. Glad to see you all made it." Dad said, "Wait a minute." and went into the gent's toilet and me and Mum went into the ladies. When we all came out Dad asked Grandma, "Where have you been? We went to the caravan and you weren't there." Grandma laughed and asked Dad, "Where do you think we've been?" Before Dad could answer his Mother, she piped up saying, "Bloody bingo where else?" Then we all went back to the caravan.

Grandma and Ada went in the caravan and started making some sandwiches and cups of tea, while Dad unloaded the things out of the car. During this time I sat on the box at the side of the caravan that held the caravan's gas bottles and Mum just lent on the boxes. I was so excited, and continued asking lots of questions including, "When are we going to the beach Mum?" and "When can we have a proper look at the sea?"

Then Grandma beckoned us all to come in to the caravan for some lunch, which was egg and bacon sandwiches and a cup of tea each. Which we all, including Grandma and her sister Ada, soon ate and drank. Grandma then said, "I don't know what you're all going to do, but I'll leave the door unlocked as me and Ada are off back to bingo for the second session."

She asked Dad to take Mum and me to the beach to see the donkeys and maybe make sand castles with the bucket and spade I was holding that my Dad had brought in from the car.

Dad responded, "Well if you're going to the Bingo I'm off to the arcade." "You can take Sara to the beach." He said to my Mum, and in a flash had gone out the door. Grandma said to Mum, "If you need anything just help yourself. We're off now." and they too now left.

So Mum took me to the beach with the bucket and spade and we made a sand castle that I was really proud of. But then I asked Mum, "Where are the donkeys?" "I don't know love," she said, "They may have gone home for the day to have something to eat. They don't live on the beach Sweetheart."

With the wind now picking up and the sun going behind the clouds it was getting a bit chilly so we both headed back to Grandma's caravan and knocked but got no reply.

So we just went in and, now feeling tired, I fell asleep on the settee. When I woke up Grandma and Ada were sat there at the table in the caravan eating fish and chips.

I asked them, "Where's my Mum?" Ada replied, "Shush child, she's asleep in the bedroom. It's been a long day for her you know." I then asked, Well where's my Dad Auntie Ada?" "I don't know." she replied. Then I said, "But it's dark now and all them sharks in the sea might come out and get him." Grandma and Ada laughed saying, "No love, they won't, they can't come out of the sea. Your Dad will be fine."

Well sometime in the night Dad came back. Singing his head off and waking everyone up, fumbling around in the caravan in the dull light of the caravan park's lights from outside.

I could see him through the open door of my small bedroom. "I can't find the light switch!" he shouted. His Mum, my Grandma, went mad and yelled at Dad, "Get to bed, you're drunk. I'll deal with you in the morning!" But Dad just said, "Alright then." Then he sat on the settee, rolled on to his side and fell asleep.

When I woke up it was to the raised voices of Grandma, Auntie Ada and Mum telling Dad off for showing them all up last night. Well when everything calmed down Dad said, "Right I'm off to the arcade." Mum said, "Hang on love, please leave us some money for me and Sara for some food and maybe a ride or two on the donkeys."

So Dad put his hand in his pocket, grabbed out a lot of change and slammed it down on the table, saying, "That should do for you two." and walked out the caravan. Grandma shouted, "Get back here you! You've come on holiday together and to spend time as a family with us. We see little enough of you these days as it is."

At that Dad came back into the caravan and sat down. Grandma yet again made everyone bacon and egg sandwiches and a cup of tea each. Which we all woofed down and then made plans on what we would all do that day.

Which really was just the same as yesterday. Grandma and Auntie Ada would go to Bingo again, Dad would go to the arcade and me and Mum would go to the beach again This time though we would all meet up back at the caravan for tea.

So everyone did as planned. Mum and me went to the beach where I got a lovely surprise. Wow! There were the donkeys, walking up and down the beach with a man leading them with a rope and children taking it in turns to have a ride on them.

Well I couldn't contain myself and yelled, "Mum! Mum! Please can I have a ride on the Donkeys?" To which Mum replied, "Oh yes you can my love." "Oh yeah!" I cried, "Brilliant!" So after queuing up along with other parents and their children, now it was my turn.

Now being so excited, I said aloud, "At last,

yeah!" But the man, hearing me, said, "Hang on, hold out your hand." So I held out my hand and the man placed some sugar cubes in my hand and said, "Just one at a time now, place one in the palm of your hand and feed the donkey." Which I did and felt so proud of myself.

After feeding the donkey a few cubes the man lifted me up and sat me on the donkey's back and yeah, away down the beach we went. I had a couple of rides on the donkeys, then off with my Mum down the beach where we made another sand castle.

But just as the day before the wind started to pick up, the sky became cloudy and darkened and it went cold. So off back to the caravan where Grandma was waiting along with Dad. Grandma had bought everyone fish and chips and buttered some bread. Then she made a cup of tea and everyone had their fill. I soon fell asleep after tea.

When I awoke everyone got dressed up a bit then we all went to the on site club for the night's entertainment. Bingo first, I found that boring and soon became restless. But just as I got really bored up on the stage popped clowns and people dressed in Disney outfits, singing all the Disney songs. I found that part of the night exciting and fun.

But then the DJ came on with such loud music and all these flashing lights. I soon got a headache as back home it was always a quiet place as we didn't even had a TV at home at the time. So when it was time for everyone to go home to the caravan I found it a relief and soon fell asleep back in my little room in Grandma's caravan.

Chapter Three
Home and Hospital Trip for Mum

The next morning everyone had risen from their beds, got washed and dressed and we were all sat round the table having our breakfast. Mum told everyone she wasn't feeling too well and she looked really pale and gaunt.

Grandma said, "I know love. You haven't looked very well for weeks now and to be honest I think you may be pregnant. Have you seen the doctor?" Mum said, "No I don't like to bother them." "Bother them!" Grandma yelled, "Don't be stupid, you need looking at." Grandma then said to my Dad, "What the hell have you been doing? Your wife looks dreadful, have you not noticed?" He just stayed silent.

Then Grandma said, "As soon as you get home you take your wife to the doctors. She could be carrying a grandchild for me and maybe a son for you. Get her sorted out, right?" Dad said, "OK Mother, we'll be heading home today anyway as I've got a new shift to start at work tomorrow night. It'll have to be Monday when I phone the doctors." "Be sure to let me know how she gets on!" Grandma yelled.

Anyway it was raining outside so everyone stayed in the caravan that morning listening to the radio and chatting. Then Grandma said to Aunty Ada, "Right our kid let's go Bingo." "We'll see you when we get back everyone." Dad said, "Take your keys Mum, as we will have set off home by the time you get back and we'll just shut the caravan door after us when we leave." "I hope we beat the traffic." Dad said. Well off Grandma and Ada went to bingo. Immediately after they were gone Dad said, "Come on then, let's get our stuff packed up and go."

So after loading the car with our things we got in

the car and set off home. But we hadn't gone too far down the main road when there were flashing lights outside a shop. Dad pulled the car over, parked up and asked me and Mum if we wanted a bottle of juice to drink on our long journey home.

I said, "Yes please." Dad said, "And do you want some crisps?" "Yes please Dad." I replied. Dad went off and bought me some juice and crisps, and a bar of chocolate. I was really pleased as this was a strange thing Dad had done. Mum didn't want anything as she said she was feeling sick and rolled the car window down to get some cool and fresh air.

Dad then said, "I won't be long." and said, "One last fling before we go Mar." and he walked off again, to what I thought was another shop. The one with the flashing lights outside and he went in. I asked my Mum, "Is Dad going to buy some more nice things for us Mum?" "No love," she said, "It's your Dad's favourite type of shop, it's just another arcade where your Dad likes to play games."

While Mum and I waited we watched all the families walking passed our car with their children carrying balloons and eating rock and ice cream.

This time though Dad wasn't too long and soon came back to the car. Then we were off again on our way home.

When we got to Prestatyn Dad pulled the car over into a garage and filled the petrol tank on the car up. Then off we went again on our way home till we got to Queensferry, where Dad pulled over again. This time it was to get some cigarettes and a loaf of bread. Around about this time I fell asleep and the next thing I knew we were all back outside our own home in Stockport.

After we had all unloaded the car into the house Dad made us all some beans on toast. After we had all eaten this, Dad went out leaving me with my Mum.

Soon after Dad had gone out Mum was being sick and soon phoned the doctor who came out ever so quickly. After looking my Mum over he told her, "You need to be in hospital Marie." That was my Mum's name.

But Marie answered him saying that she will have to wait for her husband to get home first as there was no one to take care of me. The doctor then gave Mum a letter for some medicine and a note to give them at the hospital when she would go.

I was upset about my Mum being so sick but was buzzing at the same time at the thought I may soon be getting a new brother or sister. "Someone at last to play with." I thought.

Dad didn't come home that night but came home the next afternoon. Straight away when Mum told him about the doctor calling to the house they had another row. With Dad shouting, "My Mar will blame me and moan about me not being here when the doctor called." Dad was afraid of his Mother and had always done what she had told him to do. But now if she found this out Dad would be in bad trouble.

So Dad phoned his brother, my Uncle Tommy, to come and babysit me while Dad took Mum to the hospital, which was Stepping Hill in Stockport. Uncle Tommy came to the house shortly afterwards and babysat me while Dad took Mum to the Hospital.

The Doctors at the Hospital performed lots of tests on my Mum. She wasn't having a baby, she was seriously ill. They kept my Mum in hospital for yet even more tests. When Dad returned home I kept asking, "What is it? Is it a boy Dad or is it Girl Dad?" But Dad just belted me around the ear and put me to bed saying, "Stay in your room and be quiet." Then he went downstairs to chat with his brother Tommy.

The next morning when I awoke my Dad got me dressed and gave me some toast. That evening Dad took me round to his Mother's house and asked if she would babysit me as Marie had gone into hospital and Grandma agreed.

So Dad left me with Grandma and went off to visit Mum in the hospital and find out what the problem was with her. Also to ask how long Mum was going to be in hospital for. As he had no one to take care of the home and me, plus he had a job to go to and did not want to have any time work and lose money.

Well when Dad got to the Hospital to visit Mum and have a chat with the Doctors he was shocked at what they had to say to him. That was things at home would now have to change in a big way. First of all a hospital type bed would have to be supplied and set up as well as many adaptations to our house to help Mum to get around, plus Mum would now also need a commode.

Mum had been diagnosed with Fibromyalgia as well as osteoarthritis and endometriosis and would now need constant care. Which social services would arrange with our family, The hospital would try medication on Mum to try and give her a bit better quality of life. If and only if they could lift her health up and make her stronger maybe some time in the future they might operate on Mum's women's bits.

When Dad came home he wasn't in a good mood. He phoned the extended family and told them Mum was in hospital and what they had diagnosed. Also that he would need a baby sitter and help while he would be working his shifts at I.C.I as he couldn't afford to take the time off work because he had the mortgage to pay or our family would end up on the streets homeless.

Grandma, who had now returned off her holiday, said her and her sister Ada could help out a little and good old Uncle Reg said with him being a self employed decorator he could arrange to take and pick me up from school for Mum and Dad if that would help. Then Grandma could make some evening and weekend meals for our little family.

The social nurses would help by keeping the house tidy and others would treat Mum's ailments and some toilet issues. All Dad had to do now was pay the bills and make the odd meal. The decorating would be done by good old Uncle Reg.

Over the next couple weeks all went well and Mum's health was a little better so she wanted to come home. So the doctors agreed, knowing the hospital bed had been delivered and set up and most of the important adaptations had been completed in our home for Mum. So the Doctors let Mum come home.

<u>Chapter Four</u>
<u>Mum's Homecoming</u>

With great anticipation me, Dad and Grandma watched and waited on the front outside our house for the social services ambulance to arrive bringing my Mum home. When it arrived I was so happy to see my Mum again. So as they lowered the back lift plate of the ambulance with my Mum on it in her wheelchair I just ran up to hug her and give her a kiss.

Dad went mad shouting, "That little brat's at it again, stupid kid!" Grandma gave Dad a good slap and said, "You evil bugger our Alf, can't you see she's missed her mother unlike you." I just couldn't let go of Mum as the ambulance man wheeled her down the path, into the house and into the living room where her new hospital bed was.

Then he helped my Mum into bed, settled her down and said, "There you go Marie, home now, good luck." Grandma shook his hand and said, "Thank you." Then he was off, back to the ambulance and drove off.

Meanwhile I cried and hugged Mum saying, "I love you." over and over again. Dad made everyone a cup of tea and some toast. Then Dad told me, "Go and play in your shed while we adults have a chat." I did what Dad told me to, though I really just wanted to be with my Mum.

After what seemed like a lifetime Dad finally called me in from the shed. So I ran in the house only to find Grandma had left and Mum was now asleep. Dad said, "Go up to your room, I'll call you back down when your Mum wakes up and give you both some food to eat."

I hadn't been upstairs long when there was a loud knock on the door. Dad answered the door and it was good old Uncle Reg with a portable TV for Mum to watch while she was lay in bed. He even had a remote thing to change the channels and the TV had its own little round wire antenna on top.

"Wow!" Mum said, "That's great Reg. What do we owe you for it?" "That's what families are for our Marie love. You owe me nowt, just get better soon eh." And Reg soon set up the TV for Mum while Dad just made grumpy noises and smoked his pipe.

Then Dad made everyone, including good old Uncle Reg, egg and beans on toast. All the adults started eating their egg and beans on toast while chatting and sitting on the three piece suite, because the table and chairs we used to have had now been sold to make way and room for Mum's new bed. Which was now at the end of the living room where the table and chairs used to be.

Soon after good old Uncle Reg had to go home, so he gave Mum a kiss on the cheek, said his goodbyes, waved to me and Mum and left.

Then Dad lit up his pipe again and said, "Cheeky sod he is! What does he think we are? Scroungers or what?" Mum simply said, "Well give it back then Alf and explain why you don't want his gift." Dad went silent for a minute then said, "I'm going to the bloody pub don't wait up for me."

Later that night, after I had made Mum some sandwiches and given her a jug of water and a bottle of orange cordial I went to bed and said my prayers, thanking God for bringing my Mum home and fell asleep.

The next morning I was woken up by someone knocking on the front door of our house, so I went downstairs and answered the door. Yeah it was Grandma, who had called round to take me to school. I let her in and told her I'd forgotten all about school and Dad hadn't woken me up as he normally did while Mum was in hospital.

Grandma went into the living room out of the hallway to see and speak to Mum. She said, "Morning Marie and how are we today?" Mum said, "Better now I'm home." Then Grandma asked, "Where's my Son then?" Mum said, "I don't know, do you know where Dad is Sara?" I replied, "No Mum I don't." Grandma said, "Is it OK if I go to his room and tell the bugger off?" Mum replied, "Be my guest."

Grandma went upstairs to tell Dad off but she found the bedroom empty and the bed unslept in. Well Grandma came back downstairs in a right bad mood and said, "I'm going to go and look for that boy of mine and give him what for! Leaving a sick wife and my Granddaughter to fend for themselves it's not good enough I'll tell you!" and off she went to look for Dad.

Grandma spoke to one of Dad's friends, who told her Dad had spent the night with a mate he knew from fishing. And that he had been with the same mate the night before drinking and playing snooker in the local Conservative Club and Alf had just gone home now. Grandma was furious now and returned back to our house where Dad had just got in to find I had now missed school and was shouting at him for going back to his old ways and staying out without telling anyone.

While Dad was making his excuses in popped

Grandma, and believe me, what happened and what was said was not a pretty sight or sound. When everything calmed down Dad said, "It won't happen again I promise." When Grandma left Dad just went up to his bedroom without saying a word, but he was sulking.

I decided to try and make some toast and cuppa soup for my Mum and me to eat as it was getting way passed dinner time and I was hungry. Now then the toast was a great success with lashings of butter on it and the cuppa soup looked just right so I was real proud of my achievement. Mum didn't say anything except, "Thank you." and dipped the toast into the soup. Now that was the disaster as I'd made the cuppa soup with hot water out of the tap.

Mum didn't tell me at the time and just ate this meal I had made. It was years later when Mum told me about this meal I had made and we both laughed about it then.

Back to the story now. As the weeks passed I was taking myself off to school and Grandma didn't call round that often these days, so as not to get involved in our little family's fall outs.

Time continued to pass and Dad still didn't change. He carried on gambling and staying out often. Mum and I just learned to accept these things as they were.

One unforgettable night Dad came home in his usual bad mood but this time he was well and truly drunk and crying. This was the first time I'd seen my Dad cry. Mum asked him what was wrong. Dad replied, "Our kid's wife's died." Mum said, "Which one love?" Dad said, "Our Ronald you dopey ?." Mum then said, "Aw, come here love." to Dad, and put her arms out to give him a cuddle. Dad just said, "Bog off, I'm going to bed, leave me alone!" Mum said to me, "We'll have to leave him to it Sweetheart. It'll just end in an almighty row otherwise." So that's what we did.

A few days later there came another big day for me. Now it was another change in my life, starting at my secondary school called Bredbury Comprehensive, which later became known as Werneth Secondary School while I still attended there. It wasn't too big a jolt though as some of my friends from St. Marks Junior School had also started to attend this new school with me.

A week or so later my Dad came in drunk again, this time wearing a suit, which was very rare for my Dad. Mum said, "Wit de woo, where have you been dressed up?" Dad replied, "To the funeral." Mum said, "Who's funeral love?" Dad retorted, "Our Ronald's wife, stupid!" Mum said, "Oh sorry, I just thought you would have told us about her funeral first." Dad came back, "Why would I tell you. It's not like you could go lay in that bed is it now?"

At that, Dad went upstairs, came down in his normal clothes and went out the front door to the Conservative Club, Shouting, "See you two later."

Chapter Five
New School and Making New Friends

Now along with my old friends came all these new ones. Some of these would later become my life long friends. And now even some boys had started taking an interest in me too. But with never having had boys as friends I was rather nervous with boys hanging around me at break times in the school yard.

To make matters even worse, the big day came

when it happened. Yes IT, that thing that happens to all girls at some point when the once little girl now becomes a young lady. This happened at school, in the school playground at break time. It seemed to me to be in front of the whole school. I was so scared, and at the same time so embarrassed.

I'll not say too much about what happened next or what the children were chanting, except to say it was my form tutor Mrs. Spencer that took me indoors, cleaned me up and gave me a pad to put on. Mrs. Spencer sent me home from school early that day and told me to tell my Mother what had happened as soon as I got home. Which I did.

Mum got up out of bed, phoned the doctor and the chemist and ordered me some pads. Mum then said, "Now sit on the bed Sweetheart." and explained to me for the first time about what had happened, what it meant and said "STAY AWAY FROM BOYS."

When the doctor came and examined me he agreed it was just the girly thing and soon after a delivery came with these new pads for me. Mum kept me off school for the next week or so till this thing passed. When Mum told Dad he said the same, "STAY AWAY FROM BOYS you little brat. If I see you anywhere near a boy I'll tan your ass and that means all boys." I was just eleven years old.

Anyway that week off school was pretty painful with all these belly aches and trying to get used to these pad things. When I returned back to school I expected everyone to make fun of me but no one ever mentioned it.

So I just got on with making new friends and trying to learn all these lessons, that were now much harder than those at junior school. Well they were for me anyway as I still could not read or write properly at all, though I was good at maths for my age.

During this year Dad started complaining to me saying things like, "You need to start doing more housework jobs." As Mum couldn't do as much any more and, "What about getting a Saturday job in one of the local shops? And learn to cut the grass and privets. That'll save me having to do it all the time. You're not just thick you little brat, you're downright lazy."

That was the beginnings of me feeling unwanted by my Dad, and of me feeling stupid and just a waste of space. But I had to carry on and bear up to these taunts from Dad and the teachers at school telling me I was lazy too, as I needed to catch up to the other children in my class as they were way ahead of me in all subjects except maths.

Well I just got on with things the best way I could, doing lots more housework than ever before. I even tried to get a Saturday job, asking in all the local shops after school and at weekends. But no luck as the shops that did need a little extra help on a Saturday all seemed to want boys not girls.

Then one evening my Dad came in sober, but in a very sombre mood. Mum asked him, "What's up now?" Dad replied, "Families! Who needs them?" Mum said, "Come on, spit it out! Tell me what's wrong love." Dad shouted, "That idiot brother of mine Ronald. His wife's not even cold in the grave yet and he's got himself another woman and asked her to marry him. They aren't even married yet and he's going off the live in Carlisle near her family! What about this family? He didn't think about that did he?"

Mum tried her best to reason with him saying, "Well love, you can't expect Ronald to live on his own forever and be lonely now can you?" But Dad just said, "Oh shut up! Never mention his name in this house again!" Then Dad stormed upstairs. Mum looked at me and said, "I guess that's that then. You know he'll never change his mind."

Then this new girl started at my school and was put in my class, and she soon befriended me. Her name was Sonia and we became good friends and discussed many things together. Then the subject came up about Saturday jobs.

Sonia said to me, "Well Lofty," this was the nick name Sonia had given me, "No problems, the shop where I do my paper round from have been looking for a couple of other kids to do other rounds. I'll ask my boss if you can have a job. It's not much money but it's better than nothing." Sonia asked her boss and he said yes.

So after school on our way home, Sonia took me to confirm I had got the job, which I had. Now I was a paper girl and would be delivering a paper called the Stockport Messenger. Yippee! I was so pleased and very proud of myself, and I couldn't wait to get home and tell Mum.

But when I told Mum about my new job she wasn't too happy, as she was worried someone might grab me or something else. But after a girly chat together Mum said, "Well if that makes you and Dad happy, it's fine by me." When Dad came home and Mum told him about my new job he just said, "About time too! Where's my tea then?"

I had made Dad sausage, boiled eggs and beans for his tea. I hadn't learned vegetable peeling at this point in my life, nor how long to cook them. So I just made simple meals like grilling the sausage, boiling the eggs for five minutes and warming up a tin of beans in a little pan.

Now the tea I had made him, I had placed on a plate and put it in the oven. Which was self lighting with a little button you pressed on the front of the cooker. I had turned it on it's lowest setting to keep the meal warm.

Dad got his tea out of the oven and said, "Who cooked this then Mar?" Mum shouted through from the living room, "It was our Sara." Dad shouted back, he said, "Bloody hell! Things are looking up now Mar."

Well the next evening being Friday, straight after school me and my new friend Sonia, whom I'd now nick named Spark as she was always doing something and always seemed to be rushing around at school and couldn't seem to keep still, went straight to the newsagents to pick our newspapers up to do our paper rounds.

I was really nervous yet excited. But with Spark's encouraging words, we both set off in different directions and delivered our papers. Then I went home feeling really good in myself. But I wouldn't be paid until the following Friday, as the paper I delivered, The Stockport Messenger, was just a weekly paper every Friday. Spark's round was much bigger though, as she also delivered The Manchester Evening News and leaflets, which paid much better.

I couldn't wait to get home and tell my Mum about how my first ever paper round had gone. Mum said, "Congratulations Sara, you're a really big girl now." Which made me really happy. Dad didn't have much to say at all, though I hoped my new job would make him pleased.

Back at school on Monday I chatted with Spark about our paper rounds as we queued up for our school dinners. The rest of the week at school seemed to go more slowly than usual as I was eagerly waiting to do my next paper round the following Friday as having this job made me feel a bit more grown up.

Finally Friday came around and after school me and Spark walked to the newsagents again together. When we arrived at the shop the newsagent said to me, "Well done for last week you did a good job. I'm looking for someone to do a Manchester Evening News round. Do you think you'd be able to do that as well Sara?"

Well I was over the moon that the newsagent thought I'd done well and I jumped at the chance to do another round saying, "Oh yes thank you. I'd love to do that!" I thought to myself, "Wow! I'll be doing as much as Spark soon and I've only worked here once!"

This was also the evening that I got paid for the Stockport Messenger round I did the previous Friday. I felt so proud when I was given my wages as this was the first money I'd earned for myself from an actual job. Now having two paper rounds, the job took longer than before and sometimes the bag of papers seemed heavy. But the thought of being able to take my wages home to show Mum and Dad kept me going.

When I got home both Mum and Dad were there. I excitedly told them that the newsagent had said I'd done well and offered me a Manchester Evening News round as well which I'd accepted and done for the first time this evening. Then I told them both about my wages.

Mum said, "Well done Sweetheart, I'm proud of you." But Dad said, "Come here you." So I went over to my Dad, wondering what he was going to do. Dad continued, "I'm glad you finally got your wages, now give half to me." And held out his hand. I was surprised so stayed silent for a minute and looked at Dad.

So Dad went on, "Come on, you and Mar have said yourselves that you're a big girl now. And big girls have to pay their way like the rest of us now you're a wage earner. I need the money to help pay for things like gas, electric and water that you're using. So give me half your wages." "Yes OK

Dad." I Said, and put half my wages in his hand, which he was still holding out. "About time, thank you!" Said Dad grumpily.

Following this I went up to my bedroom feeling a bit sad and deflated. As I'd already been thinking about all the things I could buy and do by saving up the wages I'd earnt. Especially buying things for my Mum to try and make her life a bit easier. Also some things like nice clothes or CDs for myself. I sighed and thought to myself, "Arh well, saving up is going to take a lot longer now my Dad's taking half my money."

Time passed and both me and Sonia continued doing our paper rounds and progressed through school, making some more new friends along the way.

However sometimes there was tension and arguments between the kids at school, as is often the case with hormonal teenage girls around that age. This was especially so with me still struggling with my school work and the taunts from Dad and my teachers.

One dinner time at school this spilled over as one

of the other girls in my year, but from a different form, named Tricia, started shouting at me in the school yard about how her and her friends were better and cleverer than me and I was stupid. Well I lost my temper with Tricia and ran over to her and shouted at her.

Now Tricia thought she was a bit of a toughie and she was shocked that I was shouting back at her, so she raised her hand towards me. So thinking she was going to hit me, I defended myself, and we ended up having a pretty big fight.

While this was going on one of the teachers happened to be passing by. So this teacher came and stepped in and broke the fight up, then gave both me and Tricia a good shouting at for fighting and causing trouble and sent us both indoors to the office.

After waiting outside the office we were called in to see the head master. He was really angry with us, and said we were bringing the school in to disrepute. The head master, Mr. Nelson, then phoned both of our parents and let them know what had happened. At the end of the phone call Mr. Nelson sent me and Tricia home from school for the next couple of days. I knew then that I would be in big trouble when I got home.

I certainly wasn't wrong about that. Mum and Dad were waiting when I got home. Dad was furious with me and said, "You've done it again haven't you. You're bringing the Family's name down, and the school's name now. Can't you ever do anything right, you little brat?" I started to try to explain but Dad wasn't interested. Mum asked Dad to calm down but there was no chance of that, he was way too angry. Dad continued shouting, "Go on, get out of my sight. Get to bed and stay there, you're grounded!" At this I quietly went up to my bedroom.

Shortly after I got in to bed I heard the front door slam. I knew Dad was in a really bad mood this time, and he must have gone down to the club or the arcade again. Just after Dad left Mum called me back downstairs. I tentatively went back downstairs, wondering what Mum wanted and a bit scared as Mum had never really told me off.

When I got to the living room, Mum said, "Come here Sweetheart and sit on the bed. I'm not shouting, just tell me what happened?" I told Mum about the fight with Tricia. Then Mum asked, "Did you start it?" I replied, "No Mum, I didn't." Mum said, "That's my girl, don't let anyone pick on you, always defend yourself. And don't worry too much about your Dad."

At this I was relieved that my Mum wasn't going to shout, and cuddled her. Then Mum continued, "You'd better go back to bed now, in case your Dad comes back... whenever that will be." I went back to bed and soon fell asleep.

The following morning I was woken up by someone knocking hard on the front door. Before I could get up Dad answered the door. Then Dad said, "Oh it's you Joan, to what do we owe the honour?" Well Aunty Joan simply said in a loud voice, "Well our Alf you didn't take up my invite to my wedding, now did you? So I've brought my new husband Ken to meet you. The other bugger was a waste of time," Dad said, "You had both best come in then."

They had travelled all the way down from Burnley. Dad showed them into the living room where Mum was and Joan introduced Ken, her new husband to Mum and said, "I've brought some pictures of our wedding to show you."

Mum knew Aunty Joan had a really foul mouth and swore a lot. So Mum asked Dad to take me out to the park or somewhere so Joan, Ken and Mum could have a grown up chat, knowing Dad wouldn't mind as him and Joan never got on at anytime and had always ended up rowing.

Dad agreed and said nicely, "Go and get changed Sara." I went up to my room and got changed into outdoor clothes, whilst Dad got his fishing gear down out of the spare room. When I came downstairs Dad said, "We're going fishing again aren't we?" and winked at me. Then I just replied, "Fishing! Yippee!" And off we went fishing.

Dad took me to place called Mellor, which was one of his favourite fishing spots. I had never been fishing with my Dad before and was really excited. When we got there Dad set up two rods, one for himself and one for me using a float. But he was using both rods himself really. I asked for a go, saying, "Please Dad, can I have a go?" And he said, "No!"

Just then the water bailiff arrived on the water. So

Dad now let me use and hold the float rod and said, "Just cast in Brat, before he sees us as I'm only allowed to use one rod on here." So I held the rod for the very first time and tried to copy what I'd seen my Dad do. But he had done it so quickly, I didn't really know what Dad had done, or how Dad had cast out. But I tried to cast out as best I could.

However, I lifted the rod to cast out and straight away the line got caught in an over hanging tree. Which Dad was furious about and he tried to free the line and float. But the line snapped near the float so now the float was lost in the tree. Just at this point the bailiff called over to our peg, which is a wooden platform around fishing waters that the fishermen use to sit on whilst their fishing, to ask to see Dad's permit.

Him and Dad had a natter about how this was my first time fishing. The bailiff laughed and said, "We all have to start somewhere Mr. Watson." Then he walked off to check the other angler's cards who were on the water.

Dad reset my rod up for a second time and this time after putting a maggot on the hook cast it out himself. Then I noticed the float moving in the water, and sinking beneath the surface. I told Dad and he said, "Well reel it in then!" I tried to reel it in but couldn't, so I asked Dad yet again to come and help.

He said, "Can't you ever do anything right on your own!" And came and helped me reel my line in. Once we had reeled it in we discovered we had caught a little tench. Which made Dad even more angry with me as he hadn't caught any fish yet.

So he said, "We'd best go now as your Mum will want something to eat. We'll call in the chippy on our way back." Which we did and Dad got pie and chips for himself, Mum, me, Aunty Joan and Uncle Ken. But when we got home we found Aunty Joan and Uncle Ken had already gone.

So Dad left the two now spare meals in the kitchen. After we had all eaten our tea, I realised I should have been on my paper round by now and I was late. I then told Mum about the paper round and being late. Mum said, "Off you go then."

Then I hurried off out the door to the newsagents, where I apologised and explained why I was late.

He said, "No worries, here's your papers." I took the papers off him and went and delivered the them.

That evening when I returned home Dad had already gone out and Mum told me all about the visit off Aunty Joan and Uncle Ken, and the lovely wedding photographs they had shown her. I listened to my Mum then said, "Do you need a drink Mum?" And Mum said, "Yes please." After I had given Mum the drink I'd made her I then went upstairs to bed, feeling really tired after the fishing trip and having to rush around my paper round.

At this point Christmas was just over a couple a months away and I had seen what I wanted to buy my Mum and Dad. I went up to my room and emptied my piggy bank. What I saw was that most of my money had gone.

I went downstairs to ask my Mum if she knew where it had gone. Mum said, "I don't know Sweetheart." But we both knew really, Dad and his arcade habit. Mum explained to me that she would open a bank account for me, so there would be no more of my money going missing. Mum then continued, "You will even get interest on your savings in the bank Sweetheart."

From then on I saved every penny I could from my paper rounds, along with the Christmas tips that the people I delivered papers to gave me. This added up to just barely enough to buy my Dad and Mum the presents I had seen and set my heart on getting them. A new pipe for Dad and a pot shire horse and cart for Mum, and some wrapping paper.

Secretly I wrapped their presents up after buying them and hid them under my bed till the big day came. Christmas Day was a good day this year as Dad stayed at home for once. I gave them both their presents and watched as they opened them. They were both happy with what I got them, which made me happy too.

I had left my own presents under the Christmas tree till last. When Dad had put his pipe in his pocket, Mum got out of her bed and said, "This is going in pride of place in the middle of the white shelf unit in the corner of the living room." After Mum had done this we all ate our Christmas dinner, that Dad for once had made, and it was scrumptious .

That New Year's Eve and New Year's Day Dad was not there, as due to him having Christmas off, he now had to work New Year. On New Year's Day about dinner time there was a knock on the door. I answered the door and it was good old Uncle Reg saying, "Happy Christmas one and all, happy Christmas to you. I know it's a bit late but I got you a present." And he came in carrying a large box and took it straight into the kitchen.

I looked across to my Mum in bewilderment, both of us shrugging our shoulders. Good old Uncle Reg took it out of its box and placed it on the kitchen worktop, saying, "Happy Christmas you two. It's a microwave I got cheap from Index. No more just beans on toast for you!" Then said, "I can't stay, you know how it is."

He kissed both me and Mum on our heads and he left, singing at the top of his voice, going down our path, "Bob the builder can I fix it? Bob the builder, Yes I can!" Which left me and my Mum in fits of laughter.

Chapter Six
The Last Year at School and its Happenings

After the Christmas and New Year were over, it was back to school, in the rain, snow and cold winds of January. Wrapped up in my bobbie hat, scarf and thick winter coat. The first girl I met at the gate was Aiyanna, a girl out of my class. We both hurried in to the school's cloak room, where we removed our hats, scarves and heavy coats and sat on the benches beneath the coat hangers. Here we chatted about the Christmas and New Year fun we'd had and the presents we had both got.

While we were chatting, over came Spark, racing down the corridor, while removing her hat and scarf. When she reached me and Aiyanna she threw her hat, scarf and coat on her hanger, just in time for the bell to ring. So off we three girls went to our class room and sat down at our own desks. Now I won't bore you with the lessons.

At break time us three and a couple more friends went to have our break in the common room, where we all chatted about the Christmas and New Year we'd had and what we had got for Christmas.

Then wow! Aiyanna shocked us all with the next news she had. Now crying, Aiyanna said, "You won't believe what happened to me over the holidays. My Dad has only fixed me up with a husband that'll be coming over from Bangladesh at the end of the year!" Well, what could me and my friends say, as we were in shock.

Then Aiyanna told me and our friends even more shocking news. She had never met him, or even seen a photograph of him, and didn't know his age. The first time she would see him would be at the wedding. "Flipping heck!" Spark said as the bell rang for end of break. Best not say what the other girls said as it was swearing. So me and my pals, all talking to each other about what Ayianna had told us, went back to class.

Time flew by and the dinner time bell rang. All still stunned, we queued up to get our school dinners, then sat at the same table with our food to hear more of Aiyanna's news. There's not much more I can say about other people's religions, beliefs and customs.

A few weeks passed and I was still doing my paper rounds after school. One evening after going home following my paper round, my Mum called me over to her bed and told me, "Dad's Aunty Ada is very poorly and lonely. Though she has her daughter and her son in law living there, they don't bother with her and just stay downstairs. Aunty Ada is now bed ridden. Much worse than I am."

So my Mum asked me if I would call over to see Aunty Ada each evening after my paper round to check how she was and report home. Mum also said that Dad had said this would be OK by him and make him happy.

Well me being me, I did just as I was asked. And went see Aunty Ada each night after my paper round for many weeks, until one fateful, frightening, sad evening.

This particular evening I had gone to Aunty Ada's as usual, made her a cup of tea in the kitchen and took it up to her. She said, "Come in Love and sit on the bed." So I went in and sat on the bed and chatted to Aunty Ada while she drank her cup of tea.

Aunty Ada was telling me now about her school days when she was a girl, and asked me to hold her hand while she was telling me about her childhood memories. Aunty Ada just stopped talking. I said, "Go on Aunty Ada, this is really interesting what you're telling me."

Then the room seemed to light up bright, and the cup fell out of Aunty Ada's hand. I said, "Aunty Ada! Aunty Ada!" but couldn't get a response. So I called Aunty Ada's daughter up from downstairs. She came up but couldn't get a response either. So her daughter and I went downstairs and phoned a doctor and explained what had happened to Aunty Ada. The doctor came out within about twenty minutes but it seemed like hours.

Both Aunty Ada's daughter and I waited downstairs while the doctor went up to examine Aunty Ada. But when he came down, he simply said, "Sorry ladies, she's at rest now, she's passed away." At this I ran straight out of the house as fast as I could, all the way home, still crying.

When I got home I ran straight in to the living room to tell my Mum. After telling Mum, she gave me a big cuddle and whispered in my ear, "It'll be ok but we'd best tell your Dad. Will you pass me the telephone?" Which I did, then went straight upstairs continuing to cry, and lay on my bed, very tearful and thinking of this evening's events. It wasn't long before Dad came home.

When he came in he was shouting and swearing saying. "What's that ?????? stupid brat done now Mum?" So Mum said, "Alf it wasn't her fault, you know that." "No," he said, "Nothing ever is, is it?" and he stormed out of the house saying, "I'm going to see Ada."

All this just upset Mum and me even more. When Dad returned home he was now in a sombre mood and very quiet for Dad. The next ten days I was kept off school to let family and friends in to see Mum and Dad and for the funeral. This time in my life is just a blur.

When I returned to school I just couldn't seem to talk to anyone for days. Then one day I just flipped, kicking tables over in the class room and throwing chairs. During which time the teachers calmed me down, only to find I'd hurt my arm. So they telephoned a doctor who came out to the school and told the headmaster I'd dislocated my arm and needed to go to the hospital.

But there was no one at home to take me to the hospital as my Mum was ill in bed and Dad was at work. So Mr. Walsh, the maths teacher, volunteered to take me, which he did. After treatment he took me home and said to my Mum, "You'll have to make an appointment with your own G.P. the hospital have advised." My Mum agreed.

After he left, Mum asked me what had happened. But I didn't know. So as the teacher had advised, Mum phoned our own G.P. who called round the next day. After speaking with Mum, the hospital and the school, the G.P. said, "We will have to get Sara sorted out. I think she has had a nervous breakdown." And he arranged for me to see a psychologist.

My Mum was very upset at what this doctor had told her. A few days afterwards the appointment came in the post. I went to see the psychologist twice a week. They confirmed I'd had a breakdown, but also that I was dyslexic and reported their findings to my school head master.

The psychologist explained to the head master that my breakdown had mainly been brought about by the treatment I was receiving in school from the teachers, that the head master was in charge of. He recommended that the school look into dyslexia, and the treatment of such pupils in the school. He also informed the head master that he would be passing his findings on to the Education Committee.

When I returned to school a few days later all the teachers were sucking plums now after the way that they had been treating me from day one. Now they went out of their way to help me with my school work. On the other hand Dad just said to Mum, "See I told you she was a thick brat!" But now both Mum and I had learned to ignore him.

After I had been back at school for a few days my friends started asking me about the previous weeks that I'd been off school. I just said, "I've not been well."

But I noticed Aiyanna wasn't with our crowd of friends in school as usual. So I asked, "Where's Aiyanna?" My friends replied, "We don't know. She went AWOL just after you did."

As usual after school I went home and made my

Mum's tea in the microwave. While doing Mum's tea I remembered my paper round. I hadn't done it for weeks. So Mum said, "I forgot all about that with everything that's gone on." And she phoned the newsagents and explained what had happened over the last few weeks and apologised for not letting him know. The newsagent said, "That's fine Chuck." to Mum, "Tell her she can come back when she's ready." I asked Mum to ask him if tomorrow would be OK. He said, "Yes, that'll be fine, we'll sort something out."

Well the newsagent sure did sort things out for me. The next evening he gave me the old round back and asked if I would take on a leaflet round too. This is where I would put some advertising leaflets in the Manchester Evening Newspapers I was delivering. Also, the houses I wasn't delivering the papers to, I'd have to post these leaflets through their letter boxes as well. So really it was the same round, but it would be every house on my round that I would deliver to. The leaflets would be twice a week, on a Monday and a Friday. I agreed as this would double my wages.

That evening I couldn't wait to get home and tell my Mum. I told my Mum, but Mum asked, "Are you sure Love, it's a lot of extra work." "Yes Mum. We'll be able to buy things we can't afford now." So Mum just said, "If that's what you want, you go for it my Love."

That's just what I did. Also, with the teachers helping me lots more at school, I started getting lots of top marks in my lessons now. And now I felt much happier than ever before and made lots of new friends at school and even had pocket money to spend. Then Easter time came around so fast.

During the Easter break I bought my Mum a large box of chocolates and my Dad a large box of Bassett's liquorice Allsorts as they were his favourites. He always had some he kept in the living room, but no one dared touch them. And Mum bought me new underwear and a new dress out of her Gratton's catalogue.

After the Easter break it was off back to school. But now things got more difficult for me, as things were more serious because these lessons now were the build up for my exams. And now after getting home and doing my paper rounds each evening, I would go up to my room to do my homework, without even eating my tea most nights, till very late. This home work just seemed to get more and more and I was finding things real tough now but I was determined to beat this and do well. In the hope that if I got good results it would please my Dad and make things better at home between us, as Dad may be proud of me for once.

So now over the next few weeks I went to school on the days of my exams for my subjects, though I was very nervous. It worked out that somehow, each time I had a three hour exam, it seemed to be really warm weather, which made things even harder as everyone, including me, was sweltering in the exam hall.

On the days between my exams, I was using my study leave from school to try and learn as much as I could for my still upcoming exams. Both from my own papers and books from the library, that I could now read better than ever before.

One evening I came home from one of my exams to find both my Mum and good old Uncle Reg hugging each other and crying. Now scared, I asked, "What's happened? What's happened to Dad?" Mum replied gently, "No Love, no Love.

Come here." Good old Uncle Reg stood up off the bed and I went to Mum's bedside. Where Mum asked me, "Do you remember Aunty Vera, my best friend I have told you about?"

I said, "Yes Mum I do." Mum then said, "Well Love, she was Uncle Reg's sister and she has passed away and was buried this morning. Sorry to have to give you this sad news Sweetheart." I simply said, "It's OK Mum, It'll be OK, we'll get through this together." Then turned around and said to good old Uncle Reg, "So sorry." and kissed him on the cheek saying, "I'll leave you both to have your time together and talk."

Then I went up to my room to say a prayer for the family and Aunty Vera, thinking to myself, "What's next? How much hurt can this family take?" I was hurting bad inside again though I hadn't seen Aunty Vera much at all over the years. Round about this time is when my Dad changed jobs. He left I.C.I. and got a job at a place called Rhone Poulenc in Woodley, Stockport. There he was part of a team making chemicals and cultures for cheese and yoghurt making.

Well it was now end of term at last and time for a

break. Nothing much happened to speak of, except doing microwaves meals for me and my Mum, the endless paper round, looking after Mum and now watching TV programmes at night together, Dad's usual moaning whenever he decided to come home and studying and reading books in my bedroom.

Then once back at school, the exams were over, so now it was time for the school leaving party. Well what can I tell you. it was a brilliant one. It was also my birthday, so you know it was going to be a real blast as there would not be a party at home.

And I thought my exam papers had gone well, so things were really good. All the others in my year were well on a high too, though feeling sad at the same time, as they knew they would be leaving soon and may not see much of each other again.

We all had fruit juice jelly and custard as you do, along with cakes, sandwiches and other party food. Some of the boys had sneaked in some small bottles of spirits too. The disco was now blasting out nineties songs from up on the stage in the school hall where the party was being held. And we all instinctively just started dancing like you do. That was until our feet lost touch with our bodies, feeling like they had fallen off.

Then someone said, "Let's do this!" And we all did the same thing. Got out our white T-shirts that we had taken with us, put them on and then got out our marker pens from our bags and started signing our names on each other's T-shirts. "Yeah, this is great!" I thought, "And well out of character." But hey, this was real memorable good fun. Before we knew it though, it was all over, the party had come to an end.

So with a great feeling of dread for our futures, we all now headed off home. Some by bus, some by taxi, others on foot, but the lucky ones were picked up by their parents. Do you remember your leaving party too?

I walked home with Spark and a couple of my other friends. One by one the little group of friends I was in got smaller, as each girl left to go into their house. I ended up the last girl to walk the last few hundred metres to my house.

I knocked on our door. Good old Uncle Reg answered and let me in saying, "Wow you look beautiful Sara. Proper grown up now ain't she our Marie?" As I walked into the living room Mum was eating a microwave ready meal and a cup of tea. Which good old Uncle Reg had made her as he was looking after Mum that evening, while I was at the party and Dad was at work.

Mum called me over to her bed and gave me two wrapped up birthday presents and good old Uncle Reg said, "Open your hand." Which I did, and he gave me a new crisp twenty pound note saying, "Put this in your savings Sara sweetheart. Happy birthday." Then Mum and Uncle Reg sang Happy Birthday together to me. Then I opened my presents off my Mum which were a packet of briefs, a bra and a pair of shoes.

After thanking Mum and good old Uncle Reg for my gifts, I went upstairs to wash and change my clothes and got into my pyjamas. After coming back downstairs I told Mum and good old Uncle Reg about the school party. Mum asked if she could see my T-shirt. When I had been and got it Mum said, "Don't let Dad see it, you know what he's like he'll just moan. Hide it in your wardrobe and keep it safe for sentimental reasons. You'll look back on this night in the future Sweetheart."

Uncle Reg just smiled and said, "You sure will Sara. I'd best be off now you two ladies, no peace for the wicked eh?" He kissed me and my Mum on our heads as normal, then off he went. I saw him to the door and he told me at the front door, "You're a very special young lady you know. God bless you always." and walked down the path. (They were both right about that T-shirt. I still have it to this day and it brings back so many memories)

After closing the door I went back into the front room. Mum was now lying down in her bed. So I kissed Mum as normal on her head and went to bed. Thoughts of the great night's party still in my head, and all the fun I'd had this night. I must have just crashed out when I got into my bed.

The next morning, I awoke feeling very sick and out of sorts, with bad stomach ache. Soon after this I was vomiting and running to the toilet, which lasted for a couple of days. This made things difficult, with having to look after my Mum as well. At first I thought I must have caught some kind of bug, as you do.

But once I felt a bit better I started speaking to my

friends from school over the next few days. And one by one they all told me that they had all had a similar illness at the same time. We found out later, when we went back to school for our exam results, that the fruit juice jelly we had all eaten at the leaving party had been over a year out of date.

It turned out one of the school's staff had noticed the date on the jelly packet when they were putting the rubbish from the party into the school bins, but not said anything about it at the time. No wonder we were all ill!

However, it did cause the school to change their policy on end of term parties, to prevent any similar incidents in the future. Their policy changed from asking parents of their pupils to provide party food and drink, to the school collecting donations from parents and pupils and then purchasing the party food themselves.

During the first couple of weeks of the summer break I could relax a little bit more now I wasn't doing as much studying. So I enjoyed being able to spend some time having longer chats with my Mum, other family members and also with Spark.

As the summer break rolled on however, me, Spark and most of our school friends were getting nervous as the day we would have to go to school to collect our exam results got closer and closer. I felt especially nervous as I had struggled with my school work for so long. I also wanted to do well for my Mum, and as I said before, I hoped good results would improve my Dad's opinion of me.

The big day soon came, on a Thursday in late August. I met up with Spark and quite a few other friends outside school. We all had a bit of chat, encouraging each other, before we all went into school to collect our results. Yippee! I achieved five grade B's, three grade C's and one grade D in my final school exams. These were much better results than anyone expected. Most of my friends got good results too. Feeling relieved, I couldn't wait to get home and tell my Mum and Dad how I had done.

When I got home both Mum and Dad were in the living room. Mum said, "How did you get on Sweetheart?" I sat down and read my results to them off the little paper the school had given me. While reading the results I noticed my Dad was writing them down with a biro, on his trousers! I still don't know why he did that. Mum said, "Wow, well done Sweetheart. You've done brilliant, I'm really proud of you." and she gave me a big hug. Dad just said, "I suppose you've done alright." But this was more positive than the comments I usually got from Dad, so I was really happy.

Now we had our results, most of my mates and I applied to local sixth form colleges for places to study A-levels. Some got accepted and unfortunately some didn't. Thankfully I was one of those accepted and I now had a place at Marple Ridge Sixth Form College, starting in September.

Chapter Seven
New beginninngs and my Time at College

Well here goes. After getting off the bus outside Marple Ridge College, I could feel my knees beginning to shake with uncertainty as I walked nervously through the gates and across the college yard. I paused at the front doors of the college and thought to myself, "Oh my word! What have I let myself in for." Anyway onwards through the doors with my heart beating a bit faster than normal.

I spotted what looked like a tutor, thankfully it

was, so I asked him where the office was as this is where I had been told to report to. This tutor then directed me to the office. Walking down the corridor without my best mate Spark at my side was really quite daunting.

But I soon arrived at the office door I'd been directed to and quietly knocked. I then heard a lady's voice from inside saying, "Come in." So I softly turned the handle and entered the office.

Once in the office the lady asked me, "Have you got your letter please?" So I took the letter from the college out of my handbag and gave it to her. She said, "Thank you. Oh I see your name is Sara. Nice to meet you Sara." I replied, still nervous, "Nice to meet you too." This lady then gave me a map of the campus, a timetable of the lectures I was to attend this term and a student I.D. card, that she told me to fill out and attach a passport sized photo to. The time table had my form room and the name of my form tutor for the two years printed on it. My form tutor was Mr. Score.

On leaving the office I tried to find my form room following the campus map. When I reached the form room Mr. Score was there and the room soon started to fill up with other students who were in my form. There was about twenty people in this form who were all there to study similar subjects.

After everyone arrived Mr. Score introduced himself and told everyone to sit down. Then he explained to the group that college was not like school and you have to work and work hard Then he continued, "You're adults now, nobody will chase you for your homework. So if you're not prepared to work hard, get up and go now as I don't want you to waste my time and I won't waste yours." He then said, "Is no one leaving then? Right, let's get down to work." So that's what we did and he taught us physics for the rest of the morning.

Then the bell rang and it was now dinner time, thank goodness. No morning break from now on. So we all left the room nice and neatly and lined up in a bunch as we went through the door looking for a cafe as we all needed our belly's filling, swilled down with some paracetamol for our headaches, as this morning had been hard brain work, ha ha ha.

After dinner on to next lecture. Maths with Mrs.

Char, which I didn't mind as this was one of my better subjects. I won't bore you with all the details, I'm sure many of you will know the routines at college. I had no time to make any friends this first day, or even get to know their names. At the end of the day it was off home back on the bus.

However when I got home I found my Mum sleeping in her bed in the living room. But the back window of our living room was wide open and the room was pretty cold. I woke my Mum up and asked her why she had opened the window so wide. Mum replied, "I haven't Sweetheart, it wasn't me." So I went to close the window, but then noticed the drawers in our living room were open and Mums TV had gone.

OH NO! We had been burgled. After phoning the police I checked around the house to see what was missing, while me and Mum waited for them to arrive. Nothing upstairs seemed to have been touched thankfully, it was just Mum's portable TV, along with some money and Mum's jewellery box out of the drawers the living room that were missing. I don't know if me coming in the house had disturbed the thief or not, but Mum thought so and so did I.

When the police arrived they said the same too. They reassured me and Mum, then took some notes and told us that they would be sending out a fingerprint specialist to take prints and not to touch anything in the meantime. We tried to contact Dad at work, and the club, to let him know what had happened but couldn't get hold of him. Then Mum asked me how I'd gone on today at college so I told her all had gone well.

Grandma came round as Mum told her on the phone what had happened. So Grandma sat with Mum while I went and did my paper round so she wasn't left alone. When I got home from my round I made me and Mum a microwave meal each for tea. Then we had a couple of cups of tea and chatted about the day at college and the burglary until late that night. "Time for bed now, Mum." I said, "Good night, God bless Mum." and went off to bed. There was still no sign of Dad.

The next morning I got up and made Mum's favourite, beans on toast and a cup of tea. Then we waited for the fingerprint specialist the police promised would call. Well the fingerprint specialist didn't call until that afternoon.

While she was taking prints from our window Dad came in asking, "What the hell is she doing here?" As the fingerprint specialist was a lady who was just dressed in normal clothes. Mum said, "Alf, she's a police lady. We have been robbed. It was yesterday and the young lady is just looking for fingerprints." Dad said something like, "What a bugger!" Then Dad said, "I'll get out of the way then." and just went back out the house.

Leaving me and my Mum stunned. Then the lady said, "I'm off now. Sorry, there's not much there, they must have worn gloves." I let her out the front door and went back in to the living room to be with my Mum, who just burst into tears.

So I gave her a cuddle and as I did so I could feel her trembling. After Mum had calmed down I made her a cup of tea, then put the things back in the drawers off the floor and shut the window tight shut. Then I sat on Mum's bed chatting about what happened with Dad and where would he have gone.

My Mum always left that window slightly open to

let fresh air into the room. But she then said, "I'll never do that again. They didn't even have to break in did they? It's like I left the door open for them." and burst back into tears.

Just as I was going to give her a cuddle again, Dad came in. I expected him to start shouting and going on with himself, blaming everything on me as usual. But no, this time was different. He just silently walked over to me and my Mum then said, "I've sorted it out." Mum looked at me and I at her.

Then Dad said, "Look!" So we both looked at him expectantly and said, "But we can't see anything." Dad then surprised us both like never before, when he pulled out a little black and white puppy from inside his work coat. Me and my Mum said together, "Awe!" Dad said, "You pair of softies!" Then he said, "You'd better think of a name for him eh? Oh beggar!" He said, "I'd best go and get some grub and a couple of dishes for him." Mum said, "You're right."

Then Dad asked, "And where's my tea then Sara?" I thought, "Sara! He doesn't normally call me that." But with everything that had happened I had completely forgotten about tea. "Sorry Dad." I said. He replied, "It's OK, I'll get us all some pie and chips on my way back." Then off out the door he went.

While Dad was out my Mum and me thought of lots of names for our little boy, like Butch, Basher, Odd Ear, as he had one ear that stuck up and one that flopped down. Then the usual dog's names like Lassie, Prince. Rover and so on.

Then I said, "Look how funny he is Mum!" Mum replied, "That's it! My favourite funny man on TV is who? You know Sweetheart, the one I watch the most. I watch him all the time." I replied, "Benny Hill Mum." She said, "Well then, that's his name!" I said, "What! Benny Hill!" Mum Said, "No, don't be stupid, you daft caper! I mean Benny, what do you think?" Well I agreed, it sounded good to me. So from now on his name was Benny.

Not long after Dad returned home with some bowls for Benny's food and water, dog food for Benny and pie and chips for us. After we all woofed it down, ha ha ha, including Benny who must have been hungry, Dad lifted Benny up and placed him on the bed with my Mum. Benny immediately walked to the bottom of Mum's bed, curled up and went to sleep.

I then went upstairs with my papers from college, as I'd left them on the chair from the day before, and left Benny where he was on the bed, and Mum and Dad to talk about what had happened during the last couple of days.

The next day handily I didn't need to be in college until the afternoon. So after reassuring my Mum saying, "I won't be long." I gave her a kiss, then went off down to Stockport. First to the bank to get some money, then off to get our little boy Benny a lead, collar, some puppy treats and some chew toys. Then headed back home all excited.

When I got home I went straight into see Mum and Benny, thinking they would sleeping. No Uncle Reg was there playing with Benny on the floor, and both him and Mum where chuckling at Benny's little high pitch bark and the way he was jumping up and down and chewing one of my Mum's bed socks.

So I said, "Well you all seem to be having fun now don't you?" "We sure are Sara!" Uncle Reg said.

And Mum asked to see what I had bought for the little fella. While showing her I asked Uncle Reg how he was keeping. He replied, "Fine love, thanks." I asked him if Mum had told him about us being burgled. He replied, "Sure has. I brought you both a video player recorder and the leads to connect it all up, but nope, no TV here to connect it up to. The thieving scum they are. But don't worry I'll get another one tomorrow from Curry's or a reconditioned one from Comet."

Mum said to him, "Not for nowt you won't. You're always there for us, but this time please let me pay you if you get one." He said, "Alright, alright, we'll sort it out if I get you one." While he and Mum continued talking to each other, I grabbed a quick bite to eat and left Mum and Uncle Reg together and rushed off to college.

Just after the start of the first lecture a new girl came in the classroom. She was just joining the college so the teacher told her to borrow the notes from the previous lectures from another student.

This new girl sat down next to me and nervously asked, "Please can I borrow the notes from you?" I replied, "Course you can. I'm Sara, what's your name? The new girl said, "Thank you, I'm Yvonne." At the end of the lecture I said to Yvonne, "Come and meet my other friends, we all meet up at the row of bus stops and have a chat before we get the bus home." Yvonne replied, "OK While walking to the bus stops Yvonne told me not many people from her school had come to this college so she was a bit nervous. I said, "Don't be nervous, you'll be fine with us, we're not a bad bunch." When we reached the bus stops, a few of my mates were there, including Spark.

I introduced Yvonne to Spark and Spark said, "Oh hello again." Puzzled, I asked, "Do you two know each other?" Spark said, "Kind of, Yvonne joined my sociology class this morning." Then we all had a bit of giggle about what the odds were that Spark had already met my new found friend in a class I wasn't studying. After this Yvonne became a life long friend of both me and Spark, as well as some the other girls.

A couple of days later I was woken up by a knock on the door. I went downstairs and answered the door. It was a delivery man with a large cardboard box. I signed for it, took it in the living room, put it on the floor and told Mum about the delivery. I opened the box and it was a brand new portable TV. So I put it on the shelf where the old one used to be.

That evening good old Uncle Reg came round, as he often did, and he set up the new TV and then connected the video recorder he'd brought round days before. Then set it all up for Mum and gave her the remote control.

College then went on as normal for a good few weeks with all of us studying like mad. Then one particular day I'll never forget, all my mates were off college that day as their other subjects didn't include doing the maths course I was doing. And this was morning and afternoon lecture sessions.

Anyway at the dinner time break, bored out of my head and sweating cobs, I took my jacket off I'd had on that morning and hung it in the cloak room. And I decided to go to the local shops and get myself some treats, instead of the boring lunch the college provided. I wish I'd had that boring lunch now though.

It was a really hot sunny day, so now not wearing my jacket, just a blouse and bra and my flared skirt I headed across the car park. Then I walked towards and down the leafy path down the side of the college storage building, that leads out to just near the shops.

After going down the path about fifty metres I reached a shaded part of the path. Just as I got to the lovely shaded area, someone grabbed my breasts from behind, forcing me down to the ground and immediately tried to put his hand down my briefs, ripping them.

As I screamed and wrestled with this young man I saw his face and knew him from inside the college. This was a young man named Eddy who no one really bothered with. I screamed at him, "Eddy! Get off me!" As I screamed this another girl, who I didn't know, kicked him hard in the head, which knocked him sideways. Which gave me the chance to get away and run. This girl said, "Follow me!"

Both running, we ended up back in the college building where this girl just kept on saying, "Follow me! Follow me!" which I did. The next thing that I remember was this girl was banging on the Principal's door. Which she, the principal, answered. Then this girl said, "Get in there! Go on! Report him, that bastard Eddy!" And then she just ran off down the corridor.

Mrs Singer, the principal, said, "My God, What has happened to you? Come in." So I went in and told her what had happened. Well, it took me a good few moments to tell her. Then she phoned a male tutor to come to the office. When he arrived she just said to him, "Go and get Eddy!" As if they knew him.

Then sure enough the tutor left and came back to the office with Eddy. Who looked at me and just smiled, just as though nothing had happened. With me, the principal and this tutor there, she really told Eddy off. But what she said to him, though she was shouting, is just a blur to me now. All I can remember is I wanted to get out of there, out of that room where that scum was.

She just made him apologise then sent him out. Turning to me she said, "Well Sara, we'll have to clean you up young lady. We can't have you walking round the college like that. But first we need to talk." Then she gave me a blasting saying, "Being dressed like that you were just being a tease to the boys. Now wasn't you?"

Before I could answer, she carried on saying, "This kind of thing will bring the college into disrepute and will have to go down on your report at the end of term. Let alone getting the police involved, then you would have to leave. Or we can all just forget about it, which I think will be the best thing for all concerned. No one will ever know, unless you tell them. But you won't do that will you? As for Eddy, he will be sorted out and expelled at the end of term. OK Sara, this is alright with you."

At this point I was terrified about what had just happened and didn't want to lose my place in the college. Also I was thinking to myself, "What will my Dad say? He'll probably blame me, and Mum would be so upset." So I agreed to say nothing. Then she left me with the tutor but came back rather quickly with a new pair of briefs. She sent the tutor out and said, "Well put them on." Which I did.

Then she told me, "Stay away from Eddy and his pals and they'll stay away from you for the rest of term." She didn't need to tell me this. Boys were a definite no no. On leaving her office I went straight home and spent ages in the shower. And from now on, no more skirts for me, I just wore jeans everyday, and a pull over.

From now until the end of term things were a lot more difficult and serious. Most of my breaks were spent in the college canteen with Yvonne, Spark and a few other pals. Then after eating we'd go up to the study room, which was quiet and rarely used except by us, so it was a good place to chat. Though I never mentioned this incident to them.

Time passed and now on the last day of term, me, Spark and Yvonne all had a chat and arranged for a picnic we would all have on Werneth Low a few days later.

Chapter Eight
Flash, Bang, Wallop and More

Well the day arrived and as arranged, me and Yvonne met up at Woodley Precinct, with a nice big bag of picnic goodies each. However Spark was not there when I arrived. "Where's Spark?" I asked Yvonne. She replied, "Oh Spark phoned me and asked me to tell you. Unfortunately she isn't gong to be able to come today as her Mum has booked to go to Blackpool with her on a coach, but Spark didn't know about that when we arranged today. "Oh OK," I said, "Hopefully we'll all be able to go together another day."

Then off to the Low we went, Werneth Low that is. When we got there we decided to take the easier route up to the top, where we would have our picnic. So onwards and upwards, following the lane rather than across the fields. Still this would be a hard trek as this morning was a boiling hot day, there were not many trees to shade under and not a cloud in the sky.

On our way up we chatted about how lovely the weather was this day and how bright the sun was with no clouds in the sky. Yvonne said, "I hope we don't get too sunburned!" I told her, "I don't get sunburned, I just turn post box red." She laughed saying, "Imagine us two later on, we'll look like a bar of chocolate and a post box!" as she went brown very easily and I have always just turned bright red and got blisters. At this we both laughed as we carried on our way up the Low.

Before we knew it we had arrived at a tiny little car park. This had just enough space for one or two cars and a picnic table. Which came in really handy as we sat down at the picnic table and had a well deserved rest and a can of coke. While just talking as us girls do about college, family events and of course the tutors, the good, the bad and the downright just bullies, and about a boy Yvonne fancied.

Now for the hard bit as the lane ended at this little car park, now it was just a steep path all the way up to the top. It was hard going, much harder than we had thought. We passed an elderly couple with large rucksacks on their backs, making their way down the Low. We let on to them and them to us. I said to Yvonne, "Flippin' heck! How the heck did they manage this!" Yvonne laughed saying, "If they can do it, then so can we." I said, "I'll bet they climbed up yesterday and slept up there overnight. Them rucksacks probably had tents in them and I'll bet they did more than sleep eh!" Yvonne laughed again saying, "Yeah, the dirty old beggars!"

Then on and upwards, not saying much now as we were really tired and out of breath, but we made it.

As we got to the top, we walked that last few metres to the monument and put our carrier bags containing our picnic supplies on the bottom of the monument.

Then raised our hands, shouting as loud as we could, "We did it! We did it! Oh yeah!" as you do. Too tired really, but not letting each other know. We sat down at the foot of the monument, shattered as I'm sure you would be too. After a few minutes, we dived in to another can of coke and a sandwich, congratulated each other for making the top.

Then we just talked about all the things we could talk about, like our futures, college, work, as Yvonne had a job herself too, and we both put the world to rights, as you do. So we thought at the time. Still sweating, more like leaking, all over. Then a lovely cloud blocked out the heat of the sun. "Oh yeah, that's better." we said to each other. Then another cloud did the same and there were more clouds coming our way, so we decided to head back down and home.

We had only got a few metres down the path when there was an almighty crash of thunder which scared the living daylights out of us. "Wow! What was that?" Yvonne asked. I said "It's deffo time to get off this hill!" We had only walked a few more metres when another almighty crash of thunder rumbled right overhead. "Sh??! Let's hurry uuuup!" I said as there was a great big flash of lightning just behind us. It must have struck the monument, I don't know as we didn't wait or look to find out then.

Oh no, it rained giant raindrops bigger than we had ever seen. So with thunder and lightning flashing all around us and the rain from hell crashing down all over the Low, believe me we got down of that Low like a rocket without saying a word.

It was still raining hard when we got to the bottom. How we did it so fast I don't know. Then we arrived at the shops nearby the Low. Where we got ourselves some chocolate and a can of coke each, as when we had legged it off the Low we had left our bags there without thinking. Whoops!

Then on the bus back to Woodley, where Yvonne got her bus home and I walked home in the now soft rain, thankfully with no more flashes and bangs back to my house.

We, me and my mates, had a couple more get togethers in the local park during this summer break. But there's not much to talk about there. Just having a go on the swings and talking rubbish as girls do at that age.

One evening just after the restart back at college, I went as normal to the newsagents to pick up my papers. When Mr. Leonard said "After your round could you please call back into the shop as we need to have a chat. Don't worry." He said, "It's nothing bad or nowt." I just said, "I will." and picked up my papers as normal and went off on my round.

Then when I was done I called back to the shop to see Mr Leonard as I said I would. His wife said, "He's in the back." when I got there. Then she invited me through the shop into their living room at the back of the shop, where she asked me to sit down.

After I sat down Mr. Leonard's wife did the talking and explained that I had been the best paper girl they have ever had, but that now I was getting a bit too grown up for paper rounds. I didn't say much as she continued, but I thought, "Here we go, they're going to get rid of me and bye bye goes my wages and my job."

How wrong I was. She told me the following week she would be opening another shop, a lock up Mini Mart late shop, down the road. "So as you are now at college," She explained, "It may make life easier for you and you could work variable hours that suit you." And she continued that having me helping her would be great company for her, and more money for me, though I may have to work some late nights till around eight.

Then she asked me to think it over and also asked if I could let her know as soon as possible. "Oh yes, I sure will." I said, "But I will just need to get the OK from my parents, well my Mum really."

Well I floated home in a top mood and couldn't wait to let my Mum know this great news. When I got home and told my Mum she was over the moon too. Even little Benny seemed more giddy than ever, and wanted me to play fetch me with him. Which was me throwing his favourite chew toy, a squeaky duck, him fetching it back to my feet for me to throw again, and barking at me with his still high pitch bark, though he was getting bigger by the day.

Then bang! The front door slammed open against the wall. It was Dad. I thought, "Here we go, he's drunk." Mum asked, "And what's wrong with you now?" He snapped back at Mum, "Them bas???? have gone and laid me and some others off at Rhone Poulenc, without giving us all any notice."

Dad was really annoyed and wanted to speak to Mum, so I went upstairs to my room out of the way. But I was listening at my bedroom door, which I left slightly open. I heard my Dad telling Mum, "At work we've all been told there's no jobs for us as the company has lost its biggest contract with Craft Cheeses."

Then he told Mum he would have to start claiming benefits like all the other scroungers around and would now have to put a claim in about Mum's disabilities to get more money. Then Mum told him about my new job that I had been offered. He said, "Great, we're going to need all the help we can get Marie. And it's about time she got a proper kind of job instead of playing with papers at that college and upstairs in her room."

Well now I got my job at the late shop serving the customers and just general work. Mrs. Leonard was a great, fun lady to work with and she told me lots of stories of her younger days and how she had met Mr. Leonard at the mill. And how they fell in love and got married back in the late fifties but had never been able to have children.

Mrs Leonard was brilliant to work for and she cheered me up on many many evenings working with her. She would tell great stories of her courting days and the fun times she had with Mr. Leonard during their days of meeting and working together in the mill, Then she would tell me all about her holiday she'd had with Mr. Leonard, but that they were saving up hard through the tough times to achieve their goal of getting married and their dreams of one day opening their own shop.

Now they had opened this second shop, she told me how thrilled she was at their achievements and just how much she loved her perfect Mr. Leonard. Her stories made me so envious of the great love and togetherness they shared. And there I was scared of boys and had never even been kissed, let alone ever having a steady boyfriend. What a beautiful character she was.

Time passed so fast and this final year at collage was nearly over, just the exams to get through. Fingers and everything else crossed.
Dad couldn't find a full time job so we had to survive on his benefits and Mum's mobility, as well as me chipping in half my wages. But some how we got through, even in spite of Dad's gambling.

Mum had been taken into hospital with a burst cyst on her ovaries which caused her to have a bad infection. The hospital put her on different medication instead of the old medication she had been on for years. Which seemed to help her lots, as many days now she sat on her chair watching TV and videos, instead of being laid in bed a lot of the time.

Benny bless him was now a full grown boy, barking at every noise outside or anyone calling to our door except me, Dad and Uncle Reg when he called in to see me and Mum. He was a really good guard dog and protector of Mum, and our house.

Now the exam days came a knocking so here goes. After taking my exams both me and Mum waited and waited, Benny too, Dad wasn't interested as he just wanted me to get a full time, good paying job. He didn't care what job I did, he would just say, "Leave all that adult school stuff alone and get a job."

One day while waiting, Yvonne phoned me up saying the girls, her, Spark and Helen, had been talking and had arranged a picnic up on Werneth Low and they would like me to join. them. "What?" I said, "Werneth Low! Are you joking?" Yvonne said, "I know, I know, but it'll be different this time, I've got a few plastic macs to take with us." "Alright let me know. Give me a couple of days notice and I'll try and OK it with Mum." Not long after we arranged to go on the following Sunday and we would all meet up at 10 am at the bottom of the Low.

On the day we all met up at the bottom of the Low as arranged, but Helen couldn't make it. So after a chat and a few giggles, up and onward along the lane, passing a group of Scouts and a few other people along the way. Then arriving at the little car park. This time round though we had to sit on the grass as there were people sat on the bench set. We all just had a drink of our favourite drink at the time, coke, then we got up, still chatting. Spark said, "Let's do this!" So we continued on, passing lots of other people on their way down and others, like us, on the way up.

Once at the top at the monument, we sat down on the gravel that surrounded the base of the monument and all just caught our breath for a while. Then we dived into our bags for another drink and some grub. And chocolate, naughty, naughty I know, but shush, us girls need a treat now and then don't we? He he. But Yvonne surprised us as she took out of her bag a large flask and said, "Let's celebrate proper eh girls? Let's have us a nice hot coffee." Well what a great idea this was, the coffee was just lovely.

After we had our picnic we all took photographs of each other, then chatted about our hopes for our results from college. We took some more photographs and headed down the Low. There were lots of people up and down the Low that day, unlike the last time. And yeah, no flashes or bangs, and best of all, no rain, though it was much cooler this time round.

At the bottom we all called in the little shop there and bought crisps and a can of coke each for on the bus, Oh, thankfully this time we didn't leave our bags at the top. While on the bus back to Woodley Precinct just a short distance away, we arranged to have another meet up the following Sunday. For another picnic, though this time it would be on the canal. We all got off the bus at the precinct, still chatting about the next picnic and saying keep in touch as we all went on our separate ways home.

The following Sunday, as arranged the week before, and with Yvonne on the phone during the week. We all met up at our college gates in Marple. But Helen had brought along the college geek, Harry. Who was brilliant at his subject, which was plant biology and never shut up about plants and their make up.

Anyway we walked along the canal towards the set back in the canal. Which was a bay on the opposite side off the canal. While walking along the canal we all took pictures of the ducks, swans and some barges that passed us, as well as each other, as we walked along the tow path towards the bay further down the canal.

I was walking in front of the group, which was Yvonne, Spark, Helen and Harry, as I fear boys as you know and he just wouldn't shut up about his plants. Then I spotted a fishing reel on the path in front of me, just by the side of the water, and thought to myself, "An angler must have lost this." and bent down to pick it up.

Just then I felt the weight of someone rolling over my back, and splash in the canal they had gone! Well all my mates just burst into laughter behind me. While I was scared to death and this fellow was splashing about in the canal. Spark shouted, "It serves him right! That plant pot was trying to push you in. It was a good job you heard him creeping up on you Sara!" I said, "I didn't hear him. I bent down to pick this up." and showed my friends the reel I had just found and picked up. Which only made them laugh even more.

Anyway we all helped Harry out of the canal. He was so heavy with being wet through as we pulled him out by his arms. After a few choice words Harry took off his coat, wrung it out and hung it on some bushes at the side of the canal towpath, then sat down cursing, swearing and shivering. Well what could we do except laugh and decide to have our picnic right there on the canal towpath.

Thankfully though, it was a life saver for Harry when Yvonne brought out her trusty flask of hot coffee out of her bag, which Harry drank most of. Then we all set off back with Harry now walking on his own in front. By gum, he didn't half stink.

When we got back to the bus stop to get the bus home, we all got on the bus showing our student bus passes. All except Harry as the bus driver told him, "Get off my bus! You're not getting on my bus like that pal, you smelly rat!" and just drove off, leaving poor old soggy, smelly Harry behind.

When I got home I told Mum what had happened and she found it funny too. Over the next few days the girls, my friends, all had a laugh about it on the phone with me, and each other.

Dad had now bought himself a second hand TV out of ad in the Loot newspaper and got one his mates from the club to put an aerial on the chimney of our house. He put his TV in his bedroom. Which Mum didn't like the idea of because when he came home, he would go up to his room and turn it on with the volume turned up to its max, which overwhelmed the volume of Mum's little portable downstairs in our living room.Finally the day to get our exam results came about.

Me and my little group of friends were all really nervous to find out how we had done. We had all arranged, over the previous few days, to meet up in the car park at the front of the college for moral support and all go in for our results together. Once me, Spark, Yvonne, Helen and few others had arrived in the car park and had a bit of a chat we all went in the college to get our results papers.

After collecting them from different desks according to our surnames, we all met back up outside to show each other our results and congratulate, or console, each other, depending on the results each of us had got. Thankfully we all got though, I'll be honest, I barely passed along with a couple of the others. But hey, a pass is a pass, we did it.

As we were doing this, there was suddenly a lot of loud noise and big commotion on the other side of the car park. Being nosey, we all ran across to see what was going on.

It turned out to be Sarah, one of the toughest girls in the college, beating up Harry, who had been with us for our picnic on the canal. When Sarah had finished she walked over to me and said, "It's alright Sara. He won't be doing anything like that to you again." and simply walked away.

Puzzled, I said to my mates, "What was all that about?" Yvonne said, "About Harry trying to push you in the canal." I replied, "But how does Sarah know about that?" Yvonne then explained that Sarah, along with Harry, had been in lectures for one of her subjects I hadn't studied, so they had become friends.

And she had told Sarah about what Harry had done at the canal on the phone. It turned out Sarah didn't like Harry trying to push me in the canal as it went against her feminist views. Poor Harry, I don't think he'll do that again either.

Over the next few days most of my friends and myself made quite a few frantic phone calls to UCAS, the university admissions service, and the different universities we had applied to. Yay! The good news was we all succeeded in getting into our first choice university.

However, we, my mates and I, had all applied to different universities in different parts of the country to suit the subjects we were going to study. This meant that when the term started in mid-September most of my friends would be leaving home to go and live in the cities where they would be studying.

Yvonne was going to the University of the West of England in Bristol, Spark was going to Plymouth, Helen to Birmingham, Harry to Salford and our other friends Fiona and Sarah went to Aberystwyth and Oxford Brookes respectively. As for me, I was going to study at Manchester Metropolitan University as wanted to be able to travel to University from home so I could continue looking after my Mum and be there for her as well.

However we all vowed to keep in touch with each other by letter, texts, phone calls and maybe the occasional visit as and when we could. Which we did and most of us are still in touch to this day.

During the summer break we tried to meet up as and when our different other commitments would permit. Then Helen came up with an idea. She said, "Why don't we have a party? Both to celebrate us all getting in to university, and as a sort of leaving party, as we don't know when we'll be able to see each again once term starts."

Yvonne replied, "Great idea, but where could we hold this party that we can afford between us?" Helen said, "Oh that's easy, we can hold it at my house, my parents won't mind." Spark asked, "Are you sure Helen? I don't think any of our parents would let us hold a big party in the house?" "Yeah course they will," replied Helen, "I'll ask them anyway."

Sure enough Helen's parents didn't mind and the party was duly arranged for the following weekend. Now Helen lived quite a distance from the rest of us and she used to travel to our college on a special bus laid on by the council specifically for students from her area to attend our college. So our little group of friends had a chat about how we were all going to get to and from Helen's house for the party. Thankfully Sarah's Mum offered to drive us all to Helen's house if we could all meet up in Stockport, and to give us all a lift home to our houses after the party.

After tea on Saturday we all made our way to the

agreed meeting place in Stockport which was the car park at Grand Central off Wellington Road. Sarah's Mum picked us up and off we went to the party.

When we arrived at Helen's house she put some music on and we chatted a bit. But once we'd all had a bit of party food and a drink we were soon dancing round the room, which had been cleared apart from the stereo, a table for the food and drink and some bean bags as seats.

Well this carried on for quite some time until we were all shattered and our feet were hurting. And we all crashed down in to the bean bag seats with a bit more party food and another drink each.

Then we all got chatting again and waffling on as groups of young girls do. We must have been chatting for ages. What we didn't realise at the time, as we were all tired from dancing and too busy nattering, is that while we were talking Helen and her brother had been going round refilling everyone's drinks as they became empty.
At the end of the party Sarah phoned her Mum to come and pick us up. We all felt OK until we reached Helen's front door to walk the fairly short

distance to Sarah's Mum's car. As the cooler night air hit us, one by one we started to feel woozy and tipsy, and we all wobbled, rather than walked the last bit to the car. Sarah's Mum took one look at us all and said, "Ooohh dear, I think there's going to be a few people with sore heads in the morning. I hope you're all OK in the car."

We all got in the car and set off home. We had travelled a fair way, all feeling the worse for wear, when I said, "Hey, how did we get to Blackpool?" "What?"Asked Spark. I said, "Look, there's the tower!" and pointed out of the car window. "Oh yeah!" replied Sarah. Sarah's Mum laughed and said, "Err no, that's a telecommunications tower!" We all just laughed.

We carried on for a few more minutes then I piped up again saying, "Uh oh, my handbag," "What about it?" asked Sarah's Mum. I replied, "It's still in Helen's house." This meant we had to go all the way back to Helen's to collect my bag, and set of home all over again. To say Sarah's Mum was no longer amused was an understatement. But we did go back and get it and eventually we were all dropped off at our homes safe and sound.

Fortunately when I got home my Dad was in bed but my Mum was still awake as she was worried about me with it being so late. She looked at me and said, "It looks like you had a good time, maybe a bit too good. I think you'll feel it tomorrow though" She continued, "It's a good job you're Dad isn't still up" I tried to explain to her what happened at the party and about having to go all the way back to Helen's for my bag, though the next day Mum told me I hadn't made much sense. Then my Mum said, "Go and get some sleep Sweetheart and we'll chat tomorrow. So off I went to bed.

Somehow I climbed up the wobbly stairs though I was feeling really dizzy. I went in the bathroom and swilled my face as I was now sweating like a pig. So as soon as I got in my room I lay down on my bed. But that didn't help much and I was soon having to get up to say hello to Hughie as they say, which went on for a while.

Anyway I must have fallen asleep eventually as I woke up the next morning and it felt like there was a huge war going on in my head. All I could do that day was drink water. My Mum and Sarah's Mum were so right in what they said. All I can say now is what I said then, NEVER AGAIN!

Chapter Nine
Woolworths's, Endings and Beginnings in Many Ways

The day came when all my friends left Stockport to go to their universities. I started at Manchester Metropolitan University studying a diploma in chemical science and maths.

There is not much I can really say about this time because it was all about getting my head down as the course was really difficult and intense. Also the vast majority of students on my course were male and I was still very scared of boys after what happened to me at college. So I kept myself to myself and just tried to get on with the course, and went home each evening to be there for my Mum.

Though I struggled with some of the work, somehow with a lot of revision and time I was getting marks that just got me through.

Towards the end of my course I got the chance to study an extra module to the course. But this would have to be at a different university. So I went to The University of the West of England where Yvonne was to do this. This meant I could see Yvonne for the first time in a good while and stay with her in her student shared house.

It was great to see Yvonne again and she introduced me to her house mates, who were lovely. When I was on my course pretty much fitted in with when Yvonne was in lectures for her nursing degree which worked out great. The university campus was just on the outskirts of Bristol, so we even got to do some of our home work studying in Oldbury Court Park, which was beautiful and peaceful with lots of wildlife.

We had lots of fun while I was staying with Yvonne, including having a picnics in Oldbury Court Park and feeding the ducks, swans and wildlife on the River Frome. These ducks and swans got used to us feeding them and decided to try and follow us home.

One day we even saw some kids who must have only been about ten or twelve years old, swimming on the other side of the River Frome. So both me and Yvonne shouted to them to get out of the water as it's dangerous. They shouted back to us, "S? Off! Mind your own business, we can swim!" So we'll say no more about it and move on. That's kids I suppose.

So off we went on our way home. On our way back we got fish and chips and ate them back at Yvonne's shared house, while helping one another with our uni papers that we had.

On another day we went to the annual Bristol hot air balloon festival. Where we had a fantastic time and many laughs. We even had a go at the air rifles, darts, hook a duck and lots of other side shows. On one of these stalls, I don't remember which, Yvonne won a little teddy which we took back to Yvonne's.

We had yet another picnic watching all the colourful hot balloons from around the world. They were all different shapes, sizes and colours. Once it went dark they did the Night Glow where the balloons float across the sky with lights and music, which was an amazing sight. As always both me and Yvonne took plenty of photographs. Before we both knew, it was time for me to go home. Back to Stockport on that long, dreaded and boring train journey. Yvonne saw me off at Bristol

Temple Meads Station. Once on the train, we were both tearfully waving and saying, "We'll have to do this again soon." The train started to move slowly on its way. We were both still waving and in tears. Then Yvonne and the station faded out of sight as the train continued.

So I now sat down, thinking about the great fun we'd had. Then thinking about how my Mum, grumpy Dad and not so little Benny were at home. As I'd only been able to phone home, and Mum, on a couple of occasions because the phone box on the corner near the house share was so expensive and there was no phone in the house share itself.

When I finally got back from my fun time with Yvonne, Mum heard me coming in the front door as Benny was barking his little head off and wagging his tail wildly, stood at my feet, looking up at me. Mum said, "Who's that?" I replied, "It's me, Sara, Mum." Mum then said, "We need to have a chat Sweetheart." I said, OK Mum, I'll just pop my things up in my room." and took my things up to my room.
Coming back downstairs, I called to Mum saying, "I could murder a brew Mum, couldn't you?"
Mum called back, "Alright Sweetheart. Make me

one too please." When I went into our living room Mum was sat in her chair at the side of her bed. So I sat on Mum's bed and put our brews down on the small bedside table that was between the bed and Mum's chair.

"Go on then, Mum" I said, "What do you need to tell me? Please hurry up though as I need to have a bath because I'm all sweaty after my long journey home. I'll tell you all about what fun I had while staying with Yvonne later."

Mum said, "Where do I start? I really don't know where to start!" I said impatiently, "Just spit it out Mum, come on." "Well," she said, "I know you love Uncle Reg like I do?" I said, "Course I do Mum. He's just ace." Then Mum said, "And he's always here when we need him?" "Yeah he's the best." I replied. "Well Sweetheart," she said, "He won't be calling round here any more." and then Mum just burst into tears. "What's up Mum?" I asked. Then I said, "You've not fell out have you Mum?" as I stood up to give her a cuddle.

She said, "No, no, Darling, he has passed away." "No!" I said, "He can't have, he's too young! It's a mistake, tell me it's a mistake!" Mum said, "No

Sara, there's no mistake, we buried him last week." I yelled at Mum, "Why didn't you phone me and tell me. You know I would have come straight home!"

"I know," Mum said, "That's why I didn't tell you. I didn't want to spoil things for you and your best friend, nor mess up your uni extra course. I thought it best to tell you when you got home. Tell me your news love." and she cuddled me. I said, "It'll wait Mum, I need a bath." Mum replied, "Alright then, I'll see you shortly."

Then I went back upstairs for my bath, but went straight to my room, dived on my bed and burst into tears. Thinking about all the fun times with Uncle Reg and how he had always been there for me and Mum all the way through my life. "Why did he have to die? He wasn't that old, and the last time I saw him he wasn't even ill." After my tearful cry on my bed, still with thoughts of Uncle Reg racing around my head, I went and took my bath. Then I went downstairs to keep Mum company and we had our chat. During which I discussed with Mum both Uncle Reg and my time down in Bristol with Yvonne and Uni.

The following week, my Dad got a brand new mobility car, which was a big estate car. It was much better than the little old banger he'd been driving around in for the last few years. He was now in a right good mood, and kept on telling me and Mum how great this new car was, it even had a built in radio cassette player.

"We'll have to see what this baby can do!" He said to Mum. Mum said, "A family trip out would be great Alf. But that won't happen will it?" "Ya never know." Dad replied. Both me and Mum laughed. "Yeah right!" I said "Um we'll see." said Dad.

A few days later Dad came home from wherever he had been and said, "This baby," meaning his new car, "Needs a good run out so I've booked us a holiday, we all need one." "WHAT?" Mum said, "Are you feeling alright?" "Yep!" He said, "Sure do. We go away to Winkup's in Wales this Saturday. So get your glad rags ready girls."

Well me and Mum looked at each other in sheer amazement. Dad said, "See I told you so!" and went off out fishing in his new car.

Over the next couple of days we got some clothes together for this apparent holiday, just in case for once it was real. While Dad now would use any and every excuse to go out in the car. He even started getting our shopping.

When the big day came we all got up early in the morning, loaded up the car with our luggage and Mum's wheelchair and we were off! Mum sat in the front with Dad and me and Benny were in the back. "YIPPEE! A holiday!" I thought, "And Benny will love the beach." We seemed to get there in a flash, then unloaded the car at the side of this huge caravan.

We went in, Benny first, barking his head off and sniffing round everywhere in the caravan. After we settled in I took Mum in her wheelchair to the camp shop to get some supplies, while Dad took Benny out onto the beach, that was pretty close to our caravan, to loose his, well, you know. Wouldn't be allowed these days would it?

When we all met back up in the caravan, Dad made us all, Benny included, a lovely breakfast of sausage, bacon, eggs and beans and a cup of tea each. Wow! This sure was like Heaven for Mum, me and Benny.

After us all eating and me washing the pots, Dad asked, "You don't mind if I just nip to the arcade for an hour do you?" Me and Mum looked at each other and then said together, "No you go and enjoy yourself." Mum told him, "You deserve it after that long drive." So off he went with Benny scratching at the door and whimpering after him.

As soon as Dad had gone out, me and my Mum unpacked our stuff in to our rooms and tidied the caravan, with Benny following us, sniffing round this new home.

Well as every one does on holiday, I took my Mum and Benny to the beach, the gift shops and charity shops over the next few days. Then Dad announced Grandma was coming to spend a couple of days with us, with Dorothy her good friend from bingo, and they would be here tomorrow.

Well we were all so excited as we hadn't seen Grandma or Dorothy for a long time now as they were always at bingo. So the next morning we sorted a room out for them, had a good clean up and waited for them to arrive, with the kettle on a low light to greet them with a nice hot brew.

Then there was a knock at the caravan door and Dad answered it. But it wasn't Grandma and Dorothy, it was a police woman and a police man, wanting to have a word with Dad. So Dad stepped outside with them.

Mum said to me, "I'll bet he's been speeding in that new car." I replied, "I hope not. It'll be a big fine if he has, and that'll put him in a right bad mood and spoil our holiday." Dad came back into our caravan as white as a ghost. Mum whispered to me. "I told you." Then said to Dad, "What have you done?" Dad answered, "Nothing. But we'll have to home today." Mum asked, "Why?" He replied, "My Mum's dead." Which was my Grandma. Dad continued, "She passed away on the coach on her way here this morning." "Awe no." Mum said. I just burst out crying.

On our way home in the car, Dad explained to Mum what the police had told him had happened to Grandma. When the coach had stopped at the coach cafe in Mold, her friend Dorothy thought Grandma had fallen asleep until she tried to wake her but couldn't. Then she called for help and a doctor. That's how the police knew which caravan we were in, Dorothy had told them.

Back at home in Stockport, over the next couple of weeks, Dad just stayed up in his room most of the time and very little was said.

After the funeral things were very much the same but now Dad spent more time at the arcades and less time in the Conservative Club, and he went fishing more often.

A short time later I had to return to university in Manchester for the last few weeks of my course and to sit my last few exams. To be honest, this part of uni was just a blur with everything that had happened in the family.

After I had gotten my results from university both me and my Mum were well over the moon. As I had passed my two subjects that I'd gone in for, but only just. But Dad just couldn't care less. Mum bought me a cross and chain as a present for doing so well.

So now full of expectation I applied for a trainee

nursery teaching job. But no, I was turned down which really disappointed me. So now I wrote off applying for all sorts of jobs, as Dad just kept on moaning about me not having a proper job. I went to interview after interview, but did I have a full time job to go to? Did I heck as like!

Then after several weeks of trudgery applying for work, one morning a letter arrived while I was at another interview, which again I failed. When I got home Mum said, "Here's another one of those letters for you love." So I opened it, expecting another "Not at the moment, better luck next time." letter. But this one said yes!

"Yippee!" I cried out. Mum said, "Well what is love?" I took the letter over to Mum sat in her chair. She read it and said, "Congratulations Sweetheart! At last, at least it's a start Sara." It was from Woolworth's, who I written to weeks before in response to a newspaper ad for a trainee manageress. "Yeah!" I thought.

But on closer inspection the letter said I would take on the role of a cashier and do my training on the shop floor. My heart sank as this was not what I had expected after all these years of college and university. Mum said, "It's fine love. Thing's will get better, at least it's a full time job and not bad wages for a beginner eh love?" "I suppose not Mum." I sighed.

Then Dad came in and Mum told him about my new job. He yelled, "Bloody Woolworth's! What's that about after all this time of putting up with the brat? Bloody Woolworth's? A ring-a-ting job on a till?" Mum shouted at him saying, "At least it ain't the dole and having to rely on benefits, scrounging now is it Alf? They're your words, not mine" Dad just stood there stunned for a while. Then he stormed off upstairs to his bedroom, muttering to himself, and switched on his TV, blasting it loudly as normal.

Now. I just couldn't help myself. My tears just rolled down my face. I was agreeing with Dad in my head for the first time ever. Thinking, "All along I had tried to achieve the best I could do, and a cashier's job at Woolworth's was my reward. Why?" Now I just wanted to hide behind the nearest thing, something, anything, and just lay there and die.

Mum said, "Take no notice of him, you've done

well Sara. It's so hard these days to get work of any kind." As she said this she grabbed me and cuddled me, then told me she loved me and how proud she really was of me. Then Mum said, "Go and make us both a cup of tea love."

When I returned with our drinks, Mum told me lots about her childhood that I didn't know and she confided in me about the early days of her and Dad's marriage and the struggles they had come through together. Which made me feel much better. Then we sat together watching a musical film from Mum's small film collection on our video player. I think the film was called South Pacific.

I got on the bus to Stockport when the big day came for me to start at Woolworth's. The letter they sent me said to get there for 10 am. While on the bus I started getting a bit nervous, thinking about how many people would be working there and the size of the shop. "This won't be like working in the friendly little mini mart with lovely old Mrs. Leonard." I thought to myself.
The bus soon arrived in Central Stockport and I walked the short distance to Woolworth's. Once inside the store I explained why I was there to one

of the cashiers on the tills near the doors and she pressed her bell for the manager to come.

When he came over I nervously introduced myself to him and explained I was there to start work that day and he just nodded and said, "Follow me then." Which I did. The first stop was the office upstairs where I was given a badge that said Woolworth's and my name on, and a piece of paper with my hours on. There were about five other people also starting work there on the same day as me.

We were all then taken down a corridor and told to go in the room at the end. All that was in this room was a table with several cardboard boxes on it. In these boxes were Woolworth's uniforms in various sizes. We were told to select the size we thought would fit and then go and put them on in the ladies toilets. After us all trying several of these uniforms on we all found one that would fit. The uniform was a navy blue skirt and a green blouse.

Next we were shown the stock room and how that worked. Finally those of us who would be working on the tills as well as with stock, were then put with a senior cashier to learn the ropes on the tills.

Once we had been shown this we started our first shift proper.

Not that much interesting happened during my time at Woolworth's, it was mainly the usual shop routines I'm sure you're all familiar with already.

However the first Christmas I was at Woolworth's was the Christmas that the Teletubbies were all the rage and everywhere was selling out of them. Very occasionally we would get new stock of Teletubbies in and they would sell out as quick as they arrived. On this particular afternoon we only had a couple of Po dolls left.

Suddenly there was a huge commotion and screaming in the middle of the shop. Everyone went over to see what was going on, staff and customers alike, except those staff that had to stay at their tills so they didn't get robbed. But even they were doing their best to look at what was going on from where they were.

When I got there with another member of staff and a security guard, there were two women kicking and punching each other, and trying to pull the last remaining Teletubby doll off each other, like tug of war.

All of a sudden this Teletubby doll just ripped in half from these women pulling it. The security guard grabbed one of the women and I grabbed the other one. Just then the police arrived and these two women were taken to the office. Not long afterwards they were both escorted from the store by the police. Well looking on the bright side I suppose at least they got a work out at the same time as doing their shopping.

Then a similar thing happened at Easter, with a few customers fighting over the last few Easter eggs. These customers were dealt with by security, who took them to the office too, and they were later arrested and led out of the store as well.

Oh, if you're wondering what happened to Mrs. Leonard, I was still working in the mini mart two or three nights a week with Mrs. Leonard, as and when I could.

This was until one evening when Mrs. Leonard said I need a chat with you Sara. Then she said, "I'm sorry but I've had to take on a young lady as a full time assistant because the shop is getting busy and I need help in the day too. And this young lady needs to do overtime to make her wages up because as you know I can't afford to pay the big shop wages. So she will need the overtime to pay her bills, and those hours are the hours you're working for me. You've got your job at Woolworth's so I'm sorry but I'll have to let you go."

I gave Mrs. Leonard a hug and said, "It's OK, Mrs. Leonard, it's fine." We gave each other a kiss on the cheek, wished each other luck and said our goodbyes. And I said, "I'll keep in touch." As I walked away I was gutted and I thought to myself, "I needed this job to make my money from Woolworth's up too, with my Dad taking half my wages. What happens now? How do I explain to my Dad? Just my luck."

The last funny thing I remember at Woolie's while I was there was on the paint aisle. When a young man and a middle aged woman had their arms full of tins of bright yellow paint. They were arguing over one tin of paint. I was sent over to try and sort it out with a security guard.

The young man dropped a tin of paint which burst

open and splashed all over the woman. She then kicked the tin of paint at the man which went over him. Next minute they were throwing and kicking paint at each other. The middle aged lady ran out of the store being chased by the young man. No doubt they got them on security camera, though we never saw them again. The paint aisle, me and the security guard were covered in paint. It took us the rest of the day to get ourselves and the aisle cleaned up with the help of other staff, ha ha ha.

But it wasn't so ha ha ha for long. As the following Monday me and five other staff were called in to the office. We all thought it was over the paint incident. Some of us thought we were in trouble for it. Others even thought we may be getting a pay rise for dealing with the incident and resulting clean up so well. But nope, no such luck. We were all wrong. We were told we were all being laid off and it was happening countrywide. All Woolworth's managers had been told to cut staff to try and prevent store closures. Oh no, now what do I tell my Dad? His ring-a-ting girl as he called it was now completely jobless.

Chapter Ten
Lessons to Lessons

When I got home very early from work at Woolworth's that day as I'd lost my job I found my Dad out and my Mum sat in her chair and Benny at her side watching TV together. I said, "Mum, I need to have a serious chat with you."

As I walked over to sit on her bed, Mum said, "Don't tell me you've got yourself a boyfriend and he's got you pregnant, please." I said, "No Mum. You know I've never had a boyfriend. I've no time for boys." Mum replied, "Then what's bothering you Sweetheart? Go on then tell me." I said, "You remember the paint incident last week Mum?" Mum said, "Yeah, I do. What about it? I found it very funny, it made me laugh. I still chuckle now."

I continued, "Well me and five others were called in to the office today and we all thought it was about the paint incident. But no, we got in the office and he, the manager, laid all six of us off and explained that all Woolworth's managers have been told the same, that is to cut staff so they won't have to close stores. So I'm out of work Mum. How on earth am I going to tell Dad?"

Mum said, "Don't worry Sweetheart, I'll deal with him. When he comes in you go upstairs."

At this I noticed a newspaper on Dad's chair, so I said, "I'll look in the job section of that newspaper later Mum." She replied, "OK love." Then Mum, me and Benny watched TV together for a while till the front door opened and Dad came in. When he entered the living room I said to him, "Do you mind if I read this paper Dad?" Dad replied, "No, I've read it." So I took the paper upstairs with me to my room, leaving Mum and Dad downstairs together.

It was long before their voices started to raise in to one almighty shouting match. This went on for about five or ten minutes, then I heard the front door slam. It was my Dad walking out again.

So I went back downstairs to make sure my Mum was alright. As soon as I got downstairs I asked her, "Are you OK Mum? Mum replied, "I sure am Sweetheart. I told him straight, he's been out of work a long time now, and I didn't react badly to him when he got laid off without warning at Rhone Poulenc, I just told him we'll get through it."

Mum continued, "And now it's happened to you just the same, laid off without warning. I told him you've only just come out of work, and we'll get through this as a family just like we did then. Your Dad's gone out to cool off and think about what's been said. Don't you worry Sweetheart." I said, "Thank you Mum, you're just ace. I love you. Do you want a brew?" Mum just said, "I love you too and yes please."

So I made us both a brew and I watched a bit of TV with Mum for an hour or so. Dad still hadn't returned yet so I went up to bed.

Well the next morning as soon as I woke up I started reading the newspaper from last night at the job vacancies section. I circled some of the vacancies with my red pen and headed downstairs to contact them.

I phoned the numbers on each of the vacancies in turn. Some of them said that the job had already been taken, others said they would send me an application form so I gave them my address. One said they would phone me back later and a few asked me to send them my C.V. with a covering letter.

Well I wasn't holding out much hope as I'd heard all this before. So I put copies of my C.V. with the covering letters, making sure our house phone number and address was on them, in envelopes, sealed them up and put stamps on them. Then it was off out for me and Benny as I took him a walk while I posted the applications.

When I came home with Benny, I took him off his lead and he ran round the house. Both my Mum and Dad were in. My Mum said, "Who's Alan? Is it some one from Woolies?" I said, "I don't know anyone called Alan at Woolies." Mum said, "Is it your boyfriend?" I replied, "No Mum, I've told you, I don't have a boyfriend, I'm not interested in boys."

Mum then said, "Well this Alan phoned here while you were out, left a number and said to ask you to phone him back as it's important. So you'd better phone him back. But come and sit over here where I can listen in case he's some loony trying to phone you. I'd love to know how he got our phone number." Dad just stared at us blankly. She continued, "Well come and sit here on the bed with me so I can listen and make sure everything's OK."

So I went and sat on the bed with Mum and dialled the phone number Mum had written down. A female voice answered the phone, but being nervous I still said, "Is that Alan?" The female voice said, "No, this is Janet, Pet. Hang on, I'll just get him.

The phone went silent for a moment, then a voice said, "Hi is that Sara?" I replied, "Yes it is. Who is that please?" He said, "This is Alan from Woodley School. You phoned earlier about a job application." I said, "Oh yes, that's right."

So Alan then asked me where I'd worked previously, so I told him all the jobs I had before. Then he asked what my qualifications were and how old I was. I told him I was 23 and what I'd studied at college and university and what I'd passed. His next question was, "How do you feel about working with children?" I replied, "I don't know, I've never worked with children before but I'll give it a go."

Then he asked, "When will you be available?" I said, "Well I'm out of work at the moment." So Alan asked, "Do you think you'd be able to start tomorrow as one of my staff has just retired so I'm short staffed? And do you know where Woodley School is?" I replied "Yes I do, Woodley School is just down the road from me and I can start tomorrow."

Alan replied, "Right, you've got the job. You start tomorrow at 10 am. Come in through the blue doors and ask for Alan. Please bring your qualifications with you. Take care and I'll see you tomorrow." Then he hung up.

Mum said, "Well done Sara! I'm proud of you!" Dad said, "I hope you're paying for that long bloomin' phone call." Mum looked at him and said, "Shut up Alf." Then Dad said, "I wonder how long you'll hold this job down for then?" Mum now glared at him and shouted, "I told you to shut up Alf!" At that Dad just went upstairs to his bedroom, muttering to himself, on the way. Then he put his TV on loud as normal when he was in a mood.

After taking so much time out of my life trying to please my Dad and trying to become something way beyond my ability, I now decided it was time for me and what I wanted to achieve in life. And what I'd dreamt about since primary school days.

That was to be a teacher, like my primary school teachers. Teaching young children and helping them through their struggles. Now I had come through my hard times with dyslexia, I could teach these children with learning problems and be there for them when needed. So here goes.

The following morning I was up really early as I was nervous and wanted to make sure I had all my paperwork that I needed ready. I grabbed a piece of toast and a brew, then off I went with the paperwork in my work bag and walked to Woodley School.

I went in through the blue doors as directed to find there was a lady there who booked the kids in. I asked her for Alan. She said, "Hang on, I'll go and get him. If any kids or parents come, please ask them to wait here so I can book them in." I said, "OK thank you, I will." And she went away to find Alan.

A few minutes later she came back with a man who introduced himself as Alan. He asked me to follow him, which I did and we went to a small empty classroom. Once there Alan asked if he could see my qualifications. So I gave him the paperwork I'd brought with me and we sat down while he looked them over. After what seemed a while Alan said, "Right, you've got the job. I'll take you to meet the children and some of the other staff. Are you ready?" " Oh yes I am." I said.

Then we went to a bigger room where some of the children were with another staff member. Alan introduced me to these children as "Miss Sara", told them I would be looking after them and teaching them and asked them to welcome me and be good as they usually were. They said, "OK Mr. Alan, we will do Sir."

Shortly afterwards, Janet who I spoken to on the phone the day before, came in and said, "Hi again Sara, I'm here to help you with your first day." We followed the lesson plan Alan left me for the rest of the day. Which flew by and seemed to finish all too soon.

Just being here in this new job was like Heaven with all these lovely children, a great boss and great staff. It was a pleasure and a treat working with them all and I looked forward to work each and every day. Each and every day had it's surprises and treats, with those kids all now calling me Miss Sara which was just brilliant.

My outlook in life was now far better than I could ever have imagined. The first Christmas school party came around so fast and went down brilliantly with all the kids singing carols, opening their presents and eating the party food we had laid on for them.

The Christmas break that followed though left me feeling empty and lonely. I just wanted to get back to my children, as that's what I called them. As these were like the kids I never had and my baby brothers and sisters I never had either. After the Christmas break I just couldn't wait to get back to my kids.

Once back there amongst them those happy days just flew by. The following Easter came round so fast. And again everything went just ace, except the break that followed. Again being away from my kids just upset me so much and oh, did I worry about them.

Later that year just before the Summer break Yvonne telephoned me from Birmingham where she now lived saying, "Sorry Sara I know things have been as tough on your side as mine, but I want to tell you and ask you something, seeing you're my bestest pal ever." I asked her, "What's wrong Vonny?" That was her nick name. I don't think I've told you before.

Vonny said, "You won't believe me." and paused. I said, "Go on Vonny, just tell me." Well she said, "I've met the man of my life and he has asked me to marry him!" "What?" I said, "No wonder you haven't been in touch!" "And what did you tell him?" She told me she had accepted and had set a date for the wedding later in the year. Well I was gobsmacked and shocked, as just like me Vonny had never had a boyfriend as she was always studying to be a nurse as that was Vonny dream.

"Congratulations!" I said, "Bloomin' heck what a shock." She told me the date and said she was sending me a special invite. So I said, "Hang on Vonny! You haven't even told his name or how you met him or anything!" Vonny replied, "His name is Terry and I met him working at Birmingham Heartlands Hospital where I'm a nurse and Terry's working on security in the car park." Got to go now." she said, "As I'm at work now, I'm just on my break."

Time passed so quickly with me enjoying being with my children. Then a couple of days before the wedding Vonny phoned me again. This time to say where I would meet her the next day and stay over for the big day.

So the next day I travelled all the way to Birmingham on the train and met up with Vonny, and stayed overnight at her place. The next day we all had a good chat and then prepared for the hen party that evening. We all had a great time at the hen party in the local club.

But some of us drank a bit more than we should have really. Then we all went our separate ways, with Vonny and me heading back to her place on foot, laughing and singing all the way there. Once there we nicked a couple of pork pies that were supposed to be for the reception the next evening and ate them ha ha ha. Soon after we fell asleep, me in a chair and her on the couch.

The following morning we were knocked up by a couple of our other friends who had come to help get Yvonne ready for her big day knocking on the door.

After getting Vonny's hair done with the curling tongs and helping her put her make up on. we then, on Yvonne's instructions got her wedding dress off the back of the door in her room. It was hung there in a black plastic bag. When we took the plastic off we saw this beautiful white dress. We helped her on with her dress, then Yvonne slipped her blue garter on and her wedding shoes.

Then all us girls ordered a minibus to take us to the church. Which soon came, we all got in it and set off to the church, leaving Yvonne and her Dad awaiting their transport, which was a beautiful white car.

We all waited a the church for Yvonne and her Dad to arrive. When they did and walked down the aisle they had a lovely ceremony. When her and Terry were pronounced man and wife, all us ladies started crying as you do.

After the ceremony we all went back to the same club where we'd had Vonny's hen night. It was also great to see some of Vonny's uni friends I hadn't seen since I stayed with her in Bristol. Although I could only see everyone briefly as I had to leave the reception early because I had a train to catch back to Stockport as I had to be in work on Monday.

Whilst on the train, I started to think about what my wedding day would be like, if I ever met a man and got married. "That's very doubtful though," I thought to myself, as men still made me feel uncomfortable if they got close to me.

Once I got home, my Mum asked me about the wedding and how it had gone. So I told her how brilliant it was. Then I went up to bed as it had been a long day. The next day being Sunday, I spent most of the day in my room, working on reports of the children's progress.

Monday morning after breakfast it was back to my lovely children. After another great day I returned home and Mum asked me how things had gone.

As from day one, each night after work, Mum would ask about how things had gone at my school with me and the kids. We discussed me and those children so often Mum knew all the kids at my school's first names and some of the learning problems some of them had.

She always gave me advice on how I should maybe deal with them, and her advice helped me so much. It was like me and my Mum had this huge extended family, which was just beautiful.

My Dad had now started smoking his pipe in the house again. Which filled the room with pipe smoke and made Mum cough, but he didn't seem to care when me or Mum complained about it. He just said, "It's my house, I'll do what I like. You two moan when I go out and moan when I stay in. I can't win can I?" But this really did annoy my Mum and me. That and his loud blaring TV when he went upstairs.

Then there were those terrible smelly days when Dad got back from fishing. He'd just dump his tackle on the living room floor and ask me to clean it out. I hated the job of cleaning out his bait tubs, with the smelly old bread paste, lumps of cheese, and the maggot tubs were the worst as some still contained wriggly maggots, which I can't stand.

These days I was only allowed in the kitchen to make Mum and me some tea and toast. As my Dad had now taken over the kitchen doing all the cooking in the evenings and he wouldn't let me, or anyone else, do any cooking. So he came home most evenings to make tea, then after we'd eaten tea he would go back out and only come home for his TV and bed. He was always there for my pay day though, to take half of my wages off me.

The best times during this time of my life were spent at home with my Mum, or at school with my lovely family of children.

You all know how time flies by when your enjoying life, well I'm no different. Time just seems to have gone so fast. The next big thing for me was this. One evening I got a phone call from Vonny, whom I hadn't seen since her lovely wedding over a year ago now, saying she had been rushed into hospital.

I asked her, "Why mate? What's up? Come on." "What's up?" She replied slowly, saying, "Are you listening?" I said, "Sure am pal, tell me please!" Vonny giggled and said, "You'll never guess!" I said, "No I won't! Stop laughing it's not funny!" She then said, "Sara, have you ever been a God Mother?" I replied, "You know I haven't."

She said, "You will be now. I've just given birth to

a beautiful little six pound ten ounce baby girl!"
"You're kidding me!" I said. "No, seriously Sara, I
wouldn't lie to you." I said, "You never even told
me you were pregnant! When we've spoken so
many times on the phone! Why not?" She replied,
"I wanted to make sure everything was OK with
the baby first. But once I knew things were fine,
me and Terry decided to surprise you." "Well," I
said, "You've sure done that."

I was so happy for her. But also wished inside I
had found my Mr. Right and it was me telling
Vonny these things. Ah well, I'm going to be a
God Mother, that's brilliant. Then I thought, "OH
YES! I'm going to be a God Mother. Oh yes!"
Vonny said, "You've gone quiet Sara." I said, "I'm
stunned!"

Vonny then said, "The nurse is coming with my
baby so I'd best go. I'll phone you again soon and
let you know when the Christening will be, OK."
and she hung up.

I was floating on air, me, a God Mother. So one
day on my way home from work I bought Vonny,
Terry and their new baby a card and present while
waiting to hear when the christening was.

About fives weeks later Yvonne phoned me and gave me the date for the christening. I said, "I'll be there!" When the big day came I travelled down to Yvonne and Terry's and saw my God Daughter for the first time. She was beautiful, with thick black curly hair. This was unlike most of the babies I'd seen before, who seemed to have almost bald heads! And what a lovely smile she had, that Terry said was just wind!

The christening and party afterwards went just fine and so fast, but spending time with my new gorgeous God daughter Ella, Yvonne and Terry was brilliant. But after a couple of days it was time to go back to my children at the school, my Mum, Benny and my Dad.

After getting home the trips backwards and forwards to the school on foot were getting rather treacherous now because of the ice on the ground. This winter was a cold one and Christmas was just around the corner. The Christmas party went brilliant and the kids at the school had made a snowman in the playground out of the snow that had fallen.

Though the snow wasn't that deep and it was

bitterly cold, there was just enough snow on the ground for the kids to make their little snowman. Then we all took photos, and the children and staff all sang Christmas carols in the playground by the snowman. Then all the children went home and after tidying everything up all the staff went home, including me.

Tired and now freezing when I got home, I made me and Mum a nice hot cup of tea and fed Benny. Dad was out as usual. Then I watched a couple of Christmas programmes on the TV, including a film, with Mum.

At New Year I helped Mum to the front door. We watched the fireworks people were setting off which lit up the sky while we said happy New Year to each other, gave each other a hug and went back indoors. I don't know where Dad was that Christmas and New Year.

One evening after work when Dad had shouted at me then gone out again I asked Mum, "Why is it whatever I do or whatever or achieve Dad is never happy with me?" Mum then told me lots of stories about my childhood and how from my birth he was disappointed with me as he wanted to be the one out of him and his brothers to make his mother a Grandmother to the first Grandson.

She also told me Dad complained about everything about me, including taking what he thought was too long to learn to walk, talk, and even feed myself. Then as I grew older in rows he would accuse Mum of being unfaithful as I looked nothing like him but was my Mum's double and even later he complained that Mum had never got pregnant again so he would call Mum a useless cow.

Finally Mum said, "None of his brothers ever did produce a Grandson for Grandma either as you know love. Which frustrated your Dad even more. Just live your own dreams Sweetheart. You're a very special human being and you'll always be my baby, you know"

Well as before it seemed time just zoomed by until I got another phone call from Vonny in hospital again. This time she had given birth to a seven and a half pound whopping little boy who she and Terry had named Derek.

As before they lovingly chose me to be the God

Mother which was so lovely of them. So as with their first baby Ella I travelled down to Birmingham for the christening and had a brilliant time with my old friend Vonny and her now larger family. I spent a lovely two weeks with them as It was the last three weeks of the six weeks holidays break at my school. The time just flew by.

Now Back to Stockport and my Mum, Benny, grumpy old Dad and my children at the school. As soon as I got in the house, which was filled with smoke from Dad's pipe, I noticed straight away my Mum wasn't there, just Dad in his chair, smoking his pipe and reading a newspaper.

"Where's Mum?" I asked him. Dad laid the newspaper on the floor and shouted, "It's about f???ing time you got back!" "Where's Mum?" I shouted back. He replied, "She's been taken into hospital. Yeah, that's right, while you've been gallivanting around the country your Mar has had a bad turn. So they've took her by ambulance to the hospital for tests and stuff."

I said, "Which hospital and what tests?" "Stepping Hill you Idiot!" "Which ward?" I asked. He told me, "A5 why? Do you think you'll find the time to go and see her? Or are you going gallivanting again?" I swore at Dad for the first time ever and now it was me slamming the front door after me as I headed out to go and see my Mum in hospital.

When I got there I found where the ward was and her bed by asking a nurse. As I walked swiftly to her bedside the doctors were talking with Mum and explaining to her the chemo she had been having this past week hadn't worked. I said, "What chemo? What's wrong with you Mum?" The doctor replied saying, "Who are you?" Mum told them, "This is my daughter Sara." So they then explained to me that Mum had womb and ovarian cancer that had spread around Mum's body and now they would be sending Mum home soon.

When the Doctors left Mum's bedside I asked Mum about this treatment and she told me she had been having treatment at clinics at another hospital a couple of times a week over the last couple of months. Then Mum continued, "Now I've ended up in here." "When was this treatment?" I asked, "And how come I didn't know?"

She then told me, "Sweetheart, it was while you were working and I didn't want you worrying as you have been so happy working at the school with your lovely children." "Well how come Dad never said?" Mum said, "Well love, that's just how your Dad has always been."

Then I went home feeling really guilty and thinking I should have been there for my Mum, just as she had always been there for me. The next evening when I returned home after work, I got home expecting to get ready to go and visit my Mum in hospital. I arrived home to find my Dad, two nurses there and my Mum back in her bed, looking very pale. So I ran straight over and gave Mum a kiss.

Mum said, "Make us a brew please Sweetheart." I asked the nurses if they would like a cup of tea as well. But they said, "No, we'll have to go, we're late already." So I asked Dad if he wanted one. He said, "If you must."

So after the nurses left I made my Mum, Dad and me a brew each. While having our brews we had a chat about what when on at the hospital and what these nurses had to say. I don't have to say much else about this conversation other than it was upsetting and I know a lot of people will sadly have had this kind of conversation and know the dread it leaves it in your heart knowing time is short with someone you love so much.

Well now back at school with my children as Dad would not let me take time off work and to be honest I needed the lift these children gave me to keep on going and be strong for my Mum. I now had to put on a brave face for my children and a happy smile for their sakes, though I was broken inside.

Each day became harder and harder, having to leave my Mum to come to work. Leaving my Mum at home fading away slowly and I couldn't do a thing about it. Then each night rushing home to be by her side.

After a few more months, a sad day came when Mum phoned me at work and asked me to come home please as she was feeling really poorly and Dad wasn't there again.

I made my excuses at work and dashed home as fast as I could. When I got home I went straight to my Mum's side to see what she needed and try and help her. Mum just asked me to make her a butty and a brew. So I went in the kitchen thinking, "How strange, Mum hasn't wanted a butty and brew for ages, the last few weeks she's only been drinking milk with her small meals." But the I made the brew and butties for Mum.

But when I came back in the living room to give them to my Mum, she seemed to be asleep. But when I tried to wake Mum up I soon realised the horrible truth, that my Mum had passed away.

In shock I started screaming and shouting, "No! No! No! Someone please help!" And ran out of the house and into the street crying out for someone to help. Some of the neighbours thankfully heard my desperate cries and Mrs. Flanagan, an old lady from across the road, came and tried her best to comfort me. Then the man from next door said, "I know which pub your Dad is in, I'll go and get him to come home."

When Dad came back with the neighbour from next door he went straight in to our house and phoned the doctor out who confirmed that Mum had passed away. Then the police came and said they would have to do a little investigation as my Mum had passed at home.

Shortly afterwards a coroner's van came and took Mum away in a maroon coloured van.

Mrs. Flanagan from across the road did a great job consoling me. So everything just became a blur and I remember very little, except some flash backs of this day until the funeral.

Mum had told me two Sundays before she passed away, how she'd arranged to be buried with her Mother who had passed away before I was born. And this funeral was a cremation.

After my Mum's funeral, my Dad went to her wake. I went home and went back into my little hide away shed, still standing after all these years to get my thoughts together and have a real good cry. I hadn't been in here since my school days to do my homework in peace at the times when my Dad was at home.

Now this rickety old shed, full of rot mould and spiders webs was my escape again, as I sat in my old chair I began to hear the echoes of my childhood friends and had visions of us all singing, laughing and playing making pretend meals. Then as my thoughts were in full swing, I thought I heard my Mum's voice calling me in for my tea. And immediately I was back in the real world, this cruel world and slowly opened the shed door and went back into the now empty house. Those memories hurt so much, so with your permission please I'll write no more on that subject.

After my Mum's funeral Dad got really strict and demanding and very bitter. Though I was working full time at my school, Dad demanded that I now did all the washing, shopping, cleaning, the gardening, bill paying and all the things needed to run a home so I had very little time for myself. But still, I tried my best to keep the home and our little family, of Dad, me and Benny, happy, to the best of my ability.

Well just what could I do or say now with my Mum only just recently passing away and my Dad still being grumpy old Dad. I felt so depressed, lonely and scared right now, wondering, "What would the future hold for me and Dad now?" So many thoughts raced round my head of the good times and laughs I'd had with my Mum. Who could I now turn to? All my friends had moved away from Stockport and married and had children of their own.

Each day that passed seemed like an empty eternity. The pain of this loneliness gripped me so hard in my tummy and the tears just kept rolling down my cheeks uncontrollably. During this time I felt my whole world had just been taken away. No shoulder to cry on or anyone to console me. I needed just a bit of compassion off someone, anyone.

Dad just got on with things like nothing had happened. He got rid of all the reminders of my Mum, his wife. He sent the bed back to the social services, took all Mum's clothes down to the local charity shop, sold our old three piece suite and took all the photographs down off the walls. Then he enlisted a decorator to decorate the house.

It seemed he just wanted all memories of Mum wiping out. I tried to save some of my Mum's things, like her Bible, her cup and her shire horse ornaments. But Dad just threw them in the bin outside, smashing them and saying, "They've always been a pain in the butt and a waste of space." He just told me to mind my own business saying, "It's my house, if you don't like it leave!"

On one of the days that Dad was doing and

shouting these things, Uncle Jack came to the house. He said to Dad, "Calm down and think of Sara." But Dad just told him to "F? Off." and threw him out the house.

After a couple of weeks Dad just went back to his old ways, going fishing or spending time down at the Conservative Club and spending lots of other days out going to his favourite arcade to play on the one arm bandits. So I just spent a lot of time in the house alone doing my paperwork from the school. I also started tracing my family tree through the online family history sites and worked on that.

Then Uncle Jack called round one Tuesday evening and said to me, "Would you like a pen pal?" I replied, "Not really, Uncle Jack." Uncle Jack said, "It's a lad I know off the C.B. Radio. He has also lost someone, his wife died round about the same time your Mum did.

I thought to myself for a few minutes then said, "Yes, alright. Go on then. What's his address?" "I'll do better than that, Sara. Here's his phone number." Said Uncle Jack and he gave the number to me, written on a Rizla cigarette paper packet.

Uncle Jack then told me he had also given this man my phone number.

Anyway Friday night after school I went up to my room with my paperwork from school and sat on my bed. I was thinking about what Uncle Jack had said. I thought, "How the heck do I just phone or text someone I don't even know out of the blue like that? What would I say? How would I even start a conversation?"

As I was thinking this I got a text message from a strange number. Who was it? It wasn't work or anyone I knew. Well, it turned out to be from Uncle Jack's friend off the C.B. The text read, "Hi, my name is Tony. I hope I've got the right number and this is Sara. I'm your Uncle Jack's friend and he gave me your number, saying you need a pen pal or a friend seeing you've had a loss just as I have. If this is the right number please text me back."

After much thought and consideration I thought to myself, "What the heck, I've already lost everything, so what have I got to lose now just by texting someone? Nothing, I don't have to meet them, just text. I can always stop if I don't like it, or change my number."

So nervously I text Tony back. Which then led to several texts back and forth to each other and I thought, "Hey, this is good."
So each evening over the next few weeks we would text each other after we finished work. Telling each other about all the events in our lives, our hobbies, likes, dislikes and generally everything about each other, even our beliefs.

<u>The Last Chapter?</u>

After the lovely endless texts we had been sending each other, Bonfire Night came around so quickly. So after work I went round to my Uncle Jack's to tidy his flat and give him the shopping that I'd got him.

A voice was ringing out on my Uncle Jack's C.B. radio. I said to Uncle Jack, "Who's that?" Uncle Jack said, "It's your Tony." and giving me the microphone, he said, "Say hello." Well not being on a C.B. before I was nervous and just said, "Hello, it's Sara and we'll speak later." and gave the mic back to Uncle Jack.

When I got home Dad was out as normal. So I sent Tony a text saying that I was home now. Tony was watching his children setting fire works off in his front garden. He phoned me rather than texting saying, "I need to hear your voice, it's far better than words on a screen."

During our chat he was telling me how he felt empty and lost, and how much it hurt when we finished our text chats. I told him I felt the same way, which I did. Then we both started telling each other how we loved the texts we were sending each other and couldn't wait till we could meet up and see each other face to face.

I said, "Me too, as I feel alone here as well because my Dad is seldom home and when he is he's just grumpy and moaning." I then told Tony I wish my Mum was still here.

Tony said, "I think," he paused, then he said, "No, I know I love you, I'm in love with you." I replied, " I know you do, I love you too Sweetheart." Tony replied, "Well then, shall we get married or what?" I replied, "What do you mean, or what? My answer is yes." Tony then asked, "Well … what do you think?" I replied saying, "I said yes didn't I?"

Tony replied, "Yes, Oh yeah baby. We'll have to have a real proper chat when we meet up eh Sara my darling?" I replied, "There's not much to talk about Babes, I know I love you and you already told me you love me." Before I could say another word Tony said, "Well sweetheart, we will have to sort out a date for our big day won't we?" "Oh yes!" I said, "That'll be really ace." Then we chatted on and arranged for me to visit Tony's house to see him and talk things through with each other.

My Dad picked me up most nights from work, except on Thursdays, but then he was always there when I got home. One particular Thursday though Dad wasn't there when I got home. So I decided to get a taxi and visit Tony.

When I got there most of his children were there with him, as he had already told them he had proposed to me, and that I had said yes when he had proposed. So we chatted with them about our decision to get married. Some were very happy for us, but two of his children walked out saying nasty things to us both.

Tony went to the door with them and he told them,

"I've only ever had one girlfriend in my life before and I married her. That was your Mum. You've had lots of partners and all I've done most of my life is raise you kids, looking after you all and your Mum since we got married. But you're all grown up now and I don't intend to spend the rest of my days just wiping your noses and being on my own. I've been blessed to meet and fall in love with Sara. And if she'll have me I intend to marry her, with or without your blessings." They walked off not saying anything back to Tony.

Well after that eventful day I went home and told my Dad. At which he just went crazy saying, "You'll not see him again. I forbid it." So from now on it was really difficult to get to see Tony and I just went to see him when Dad wasn't at home.

Christmas that year was a real drag, not getting to see the man I loved. New Year was just as bad. Dad seemed to stay home on my days off work, so it was a hard time for us both as I could only get to see Tony on short visits on Thurdays after work so Dad didn't find out.

Then one day in March my Dad went fishing for

the day early in the morning, so here was my chance to have a proper visit with Tony. So I phoned Tony to ask if it would be OK for me to call that day. He said, "Yes of course it is Darling." So off I set in a taxi.

When I got there it was Tony's birthday. I didn't know and he hadn't said. Most of his kids were there when I arrived and stayed while we talked. Then Tony made everyone a cup of tea.

When he came back into the living room one of his daughters said. "I have some news for you Dad." "What's that?" Tony asked her. She told him she had taken a pregnancy test that morning and she was pregnant. Then she showed me and Tony her test kit. Tony said, "Congratulations Babe! But I thought your husband didn't want any more kids yet. That he wants to get a mortgage first?" She replied, "He doesn't but ..."

As she said "but" there was a knock on the small living room window at the front. Tony could see through the lace curtain that it was her husband. So his daughter asked me to hide her kit while Tony answered the door. So I put it in my handbag. When Tony came back in the living room with his daughter's husband we all just chatted for a few minutes, then his daughter and her husband left.

This left me, Tony, his other daughter, her husband and their children in the living room. Then they went to their rooms upstairs where they lived and slept.

Then it was just me and Tony in the living room. Now, at last we could have a cuddle and chat. Which we did and arranged to get married the next September, on the 26th. As this was my Mum's birthday so that would be my tribute to my late Mum.

Then it was time to go. But this time when saying my goodbyes to Tony he gave me a kiss. Yes, a kiss on the lips. So what could I do except return mine. After about, well a while, we finally took a breath. Just as my taxi arrived to take me back to my dreaded Dad's, and my, home.

Waving from through the taxi window, excited and full of joy, I went home. There I found my Dad in a right mood, moaning and saying, "Where do you think you've been?" So I told him. He said, "Well what about the cleaning, shopping and my bloody tea!"

I said, "Dad, I'm 32 years old. I don't go clubbing it or staying away from home most nights, like you have done all my life, just coming home when you feel like it. You and Mum must have dated to get married. And now even all my friends are all married. Wake up Dad and smell the coffee! I'm 32 and I've found the man I want to be with for the rest of my life. I don't want to grow in to an old maid with just a cat for company."

Dad replied, "When I'm gone you'll get everything I've worked for all my life, including this house." I said, "Dad, oh Dad, I can't cuddle up with and chat to bricks and mortar now can I?" He just told me to "P? off." Then he went out, slamming the front door.

I went to my room thinking on this evening's events, happier than I had ever been. Not just with getting married, but because for once I'd stood up to my Dad, telling him how things were, not how he thinks they should be, with everything, and everyone revolving around him and what he wants. "About time too." I said to myself.

Once in my room, I filled my diary in, writing down what had happened that day. I was thinking about our wedding and how I would have loved my best ever friend any girl could wish for, my dear old loving Mum, to be there.

I must have fallen asleep as I woke up the next morning to the sound of my alarm clock going off. I was fully dressed on top of my bed but freezing. I just went downstairs made myself piece of toast, grabbed my work bag and went down to the shops near our house and got some crisps and juice for the bus ride to work.

Once at work I just got on with things as normal, but was walking around like I was in a dream, thinking about my love Tony. Just before lunch break my mobile phone rang. I rushed over to my cupboard where I stored my things as fast as I could. "It must be my love Tony." I thought. But no, it was my Dad on the phone, shouting like a wild man.

What he had to say shocked me. He called me a dirty little slut and said, "You're going to need a really good excuse for this when you get home." I said, "For what? What are you talking about?"

Dad continued screaming, "Me and our kid Jack have been through all your stuff in your room and found it in your handbag!" I said, "Found what? I don't know what you're talking about!" He raved on, "You and that B??? have been and done it now haven't you?"

Confused I said, "What have me and Tony done?" Dad said, "Don't play silly games! Me and our kid found that pregnancy test kit in your bag." I said, "Dad, that's not mine. I'd forgotten all about that, it's Tony's daughter's! You know I only take that handbag out on special occasions, like visiting people, including Tony. Maybe if you paid more attention to me, you'd know that!" He said, "Exactly, that proves it. You're just a prostitute. Don't you ever come back here!" I said, "Don't worry I won't." And I hung up.

A few minutes later the lunch break bell went. I made my excuses and I left the school. Then I went straight to the local railway line, where I knew a large freight train passed regularly. I waited for the train and I was going to throw myself under the next train that would come along.

So while stood by the train lines a thought came in

to my head, "What the hell am I doing? I've got a future husband waiting for me. I love him and he loves me." So I walked back up the embankment thinking, "My Dad has never treated me like a daughter, nor has he ever been a proper Dad to me."

Once back on the road side I phoned Tony and said, "You know that visit I'm coming on, can I come early?" Tony said, "You can come any time you like." I said, "No, I need to tell you something." Tony said, "Don't tell me, you don't want to marry me, you've changed your mind?"

I said, "Nothing like that." Then I explained what had happened on the phone between me and my Dad. Tony said, "It's OK, come home here Sweetheart. There's always a home for you here." So I then walked to the nearest taxi company, feeling scared all the way that my Dad may see me and ordered a taxi to take me to Tony's.

On the way to Tony's the taxi driver seemed concerned about me and asked me, "What's the matter?" I said, "I'm going to my Fiance's house." "But why are you crying then?" The taxi driver asked. I just said, "Some of my family don't agree with it, it's a long story." At this the taxi driver took the hint and didn't ask any more questions.

When we finally got to Tony's house Tony was in his front garden waiting for me. He greeted me and took me straight indoors in to his house and said, "Don't worry my love, everything will work itself out." I said, "But I haven't got anything love, except what I stand in and my work bag." Tony said, "I've told you, everything will work out just fine."

Which it did. As over the next few months Tony provided everything I needed and he said from day one, "My home is your home Sara."
After me moving in, within days my Dad sent the police round saying, "I'm a missing person and Tony had kidnapped me." He got Tony's address and phone number out of my little diary in my handbag I'd left at Dad's house.

So the police questioned us both. We showed them the texts that we both had on our phones from my Dad, threatening us with various things he was going to do. The police told us, "Our impression of your Dad, after speaking with him, is that he seems to be a bit of a control freak. Our advice is if he keeps phoning you, texting you, or anything else with threats, like he has done before, report it to us and we'll go back and have a chat with him." They gave us an incident number and left to go back and have a word with my Dad.

Anyway the nasty texts continued, along with nasty letters now, from both my Dad and his brother, my Uncle Jack. Which we still have in a drawer upstairs. We didn't report them as he was still my Dad and we didn't want to get him in trouble and we hoped he'd come around to the idea we were going to be married.

The police came a couple of more times after that after reports from my Dad. On their last visit they said they would tell my Dad he was wasting police time and they would charge him with that and related offences if he sent them on any more wild goose chases. It was then that these texts and letters stopped.

I settled in at Tony's house, though I found it a bit difficult for the first few weeks. As I had been used to being at home with just my Mum for company when I came in from work, and the occasional out bursts from my Dad when he came home. But this house was rather busy with me and Tony, his daughter, her husband and their four kids. They were living with Tony as they had gone homeless last summer and moved in with Tony.

Anyway our big day was getting closer, so we sent out our invites. We had brought the wedding date forward to May, in the registrar rather than what we had planned at the church, St. Anthony's, in September. We did this due to all the problems we were having with my family. Also because I was sleeping in Tony's bed in the front bedroom upstairs, and Tony was sleeping on the settee in the living room downstairs. Tony's daughter, her husband and their kids were sleeping in their rooms upstairs.

We even sent an invite to my Dad, asking him to invite all the family members he thought might come. I also invited my old mate Yvonne, and asked her if she would be my maid of honour. She replied, "It would be my pleasure." Tony also sent his invites out to many of his family members, including his brothers and sisters, and all his children, who were married now with children of their own.

Not long after this I went to buy my wedding dress. I chose to buy my dress on my late Grandma's birthday as my tribute to her. My mate Yvonne came with me as maid of honour to help me try the dresses on, and of course to give her honest opinion on them. She came up from Birmingham where she was living to our house, then drove us both in to Central Manchester.

We looked in a few bridal shops but there was nothing I really liked or thought would suit me. "What now?" I said to Yvonne, "I really need to find the right dress." Yvonne replied, "We could try in there." and pointed to Monsoon.

So we went in and straight to the bridal department. I tried another couple of dresses on but they just weren't right. But with the next dress I tried on, me and Yvonne said, "That's it!" straight away. They also had a little lace jacket, bridal shoes and a tiara that went perfectly with my dress. Yvonne then drove us both, really happy, excited and relieved, back to our house and Tony.

Our big day finally came and it was a fantastic special day for me and Tony which we'll never forget. But sadly most of the people we had invited didn't turn up for our wedding. All of my family, including my Dad, all but of one of Tony's brothers and sisters, and two of his children didn't attend our wedding.

The two of Tony's children who didn't come to our wedding were the same two that walked out on Tony when he explained to them we were going to get married. Tony's eldest son was his Best Man and Yvonne was my Maid of honour.

After the lovely ceremony and lots of photos being taken, we went back to Tony's house where we had laid on a reception with plenty of food and booze, and a big karaoke system for everyone to have a good sing song. Tony's two children, who had been missing at the wedding, turned up for this reception.

When Tony asked them why they hadn't come to the wedding, they told us they had missed the bus. Arh well, we can't say there'll always be another day because there just won't. Some friends of both mine and Tony's also came to our reception.

So after a great night when everyone had had their fill of food and booze and a good sing song, the house started to empty. Until there was just me, Tony, and Tony's daughter, her husband and their kids who lived with us.

Then they told us they had arranged to stay out over night at another family member's house so we could consummate our marriage in peace. So after they left we made a couple of cups of coffee each and took them upstairs with us, to do what newlyweds do. I put my drinks on my side of the bed and Tony put his drinks on his side, while giggling and looking at each other.

Then Tony left the bedroom while I undressed and put my nightie on, and Tony went and undressed in the bathroom and put his shorts and pyjama jacket on. While I waited ever so nervously. He entered the bedroom, picked up two of the coffees, gave me a cup and we both had a drink of coffee, giggling nervously.

After drinking one cup of coffee each while chatting about the day, we decided to get in to bed together.

We pulled the duvet back and we gently kissed for a while, which turned in to passionate kissing, and

I'M SURE YOU'RE BIG ENOUGH AND OLD ENOUGH TO USE YOUR IMAGINATION, THIS BOOK ISN'T ONE OF THEM KIND OF BOOKS.
HA HA HA...ONLY KIDDING

Hope you like my story of a Stockport lass, born and bred. If so, please let my publisher know, or write a me review, as it'll encourage me to continue writing where I left off, maybe in a second book.

Until then, please take care, but live life to the full.

Other books by this publisher you may be interested in:

Be Home Before it Gets Dark Son by Tony Ratcliff,
ISBN: 978 1 5272 3808 4
The Sky is my Witness, It Saw it All, by Tony Ratcliff
and guest author Sara Ratcliff,
ISBN: 978 1 5272 3911 1
Manchester..More of my Life's Stories by Tony
Ratcliff
ISBN: 978 1 5272 7484 6
Obtainable from Marie Curtis Publications
email: mariecurtispublications@outlook.com
or from Waterstones online.